TRANSFORM

THROUGH

PURPOSE

YOUR PATH TO LIVING AN
AUTHENTIC AND INTENTIONAL LIFE

TRANSFORM

THROUGH

PURPOSE

REED NYFFELER

GREENLEAF
BOOK GROUP PRESS

Published by Greenleaf Book Group Press
Austin, Texas
www.gbgpress.com

Distributed by Greenleaf Book Group

For ordering information or special discounts for bulk purchases, please contact Greenleaf Book Group at PO Box 91869, Austin, TX 78709, 512.891.6100.

Design and composition by Greenleaf Book Group
Cover design by Greenleaf Book Group

Publisher's Cataloging-in-Publication data is available.

Print ISBN: 979-8-88645-271-6

eBook ISBN: 979-8-88645-272-3

To offset the number of trees consumed in the printing of our books, Greenleaf donates a portion of the proceeds from each printing to the Arbor Day Foundation. Greenleaf Book Group has replaced over 50,000 trees since 2007.

Printed in the United States of America on acid-free paper

24 25 26 27 28 29 30 31   10 9 8 7 6 5 4 3 2 1

First Edition

This book is dedicated to YOU
—the readers—who want to leave a legacy
and transform through purpose.

CONTENTS

Preface

One cannot live a life *of* purpose without living a life *on* purpose. It is with this premise that I have chosen to live my life for the last thirty years. This book is not a biography of my own life and work. However, I share some personal vignettes, so you have a peek at my own journey of discovering and living a life on purpose as a person of faith, a husband, a dad, and as CEO of Signal—a growing, global franchise security services firm based in Omaha, Nebraska.

Like many people, when I was growing up, I struggled with insecurity and uncertainty, and I lacked a sense of belonging. It was tough to find my place in school, sports, and my peer groups. I didn't really align with the ideas and vision of superiors or the leaders around me either. This book is for those who are wrestling with a sense of discontentment, feeling like you do not belong. It is also for those who are ready to experience more and do more with the one life they've been gifted but are not exactly sure how to begin.

Ultimately, I made a choice to look at my life in the long term. I created a framework to inform the way I lived and structured my life

—an eternal, transcendent, and universally applicable purpose—to guide and inform decisions in each area of my life. I believe each person has unique gifts and talents and has been created for their own purpose. You, too, can figure out your purpose, pursue that purpose, and leave a meaningful legacy for those you love!

In my life, my purpose and focus became clear as I was led to a relationship with the eternal, transcendent, and universal God. My eyes were opened, and I came to believe that a life on purpose is not only possible, but it is what we were designed for, and there are ways you can learn to live the purposeful life that God intends for you to live.

Some people may fear they will choose the wrong purpose for their lives. I'd suggest that you should be more concerned about failing to live with no greater purpose in mind. Do not get stuck feeling afraid. Instead, get busy reflecting on what matters to you. This book will lead you through an approach that will equip you to take the steps needed to live your life of purpose *on* purpose! Humans are uniquely positioned with the capacity to make choices about who we will be and what we will become. It is both a gift and a curse. This world often presents myriad options that can confuse and distract. As a result, many people live what I call a "default life."

Living a default life means making momentary decisions with little regard for the future, the consequences, or the impact. Sometimes those decisions are made to satisfy short-term needs and wants or to create fleeting positive emotions that are not fulfilling in the long run. People succumb to the pressures of culture, the expectations of others, and simply default to the easiest decisions with the least resistance. That might work for a while, but it results in a less fulfilling life—one that leaves you wishing for something more.

You don't have to live your life that way. You can live a more fulfilling life by living the purposeful life you were created to live. There is purposeful design in everything around us, and you also were designed to live purposefully.

I wrote this book, in part, to live out my own purpose, which, in my own words, is "through intuitive interaction, to propel leaders through their self-imposed barriers to live out their unique purpose in life." You have a unique purpose, and if you feel like you are bumping into barriers that are slowing your progress, I hope you will find some ideas and practices that will equip you to break through those barriers, so you can make progress on your purpose.

This book imparts principles and a practical approach that will help you discover your unique purpose and help you to fulfill it every moment, day, and year of your life! Living your life on purpose will fuel your passions and renew your energy to share these principles with others around you. It may take you some time to get started, and it may take time to learn to support others on their own journeys. That is okay! Be patient because learning, healing, and creating new habits of mind and action take time to shift. But you can do it!

This book is ordered to help you build the foundation for discovering your purpose so you are better positioned to live it out. First, clarify your priorities. This is an important first step to avoiding the default life and living your life on purpose, so it is important you don't skip it. Then, you will learn to examine and create positive habits so you can apply them to what is most important to you. You'll then take steps to know your eternal, transcendent, and universally applicable purpose.

Once you know your purpose, you begin the journey of living it. This is where the proverbial rubber meets the road. You should be prepared for some resistance and respond by creating a motivating, long-term vision with a plan to progress. You will start by focusing on the long term, but you will also learn the importance of having interim milestones and practicing those habits that help you live your life on purpose each day and each moment.

Finally, the last section of the book is about leaving a legacy. As you live your life on purpose, you can build a positive legacy that helps and enables future generations. You can make choices—big and small—every moment, every day, and every year—that make a positive, enduring difference for others.

I hope this book inspires you, but I also hope it transforms and equips you to live your life of purpose on purpose.

—REED

Establish Priorities for Your Life

A life on purpose begins with knowing and pursuing your top priorities. Not only is it critical to delineate your priorities, but it is also important to determine whether they align with the way you use your time and energy. It is easy to fool yourself into thinking that identifying and stating your top priorities equates to honoring them. You must examine whether your stated priorities are reflected in your actions. If your priorities and actions are misaligned, the lack of authenticity can damage your reputation and erode the trust of family, friends, or colleagues.

Here, you will be challenged to examine your priorities. Consider whether they are in default mode, in which your time and energy are spent without much thought or intentionality. Then analyze whether your time, energy, and attention provide evidence that you are, in practice, honoring your top priorities. You will be reminded that your priorities, by definition, are ordered. Clear, well-ordered priorities can serve you well, informing your daily and future decisions and plans.

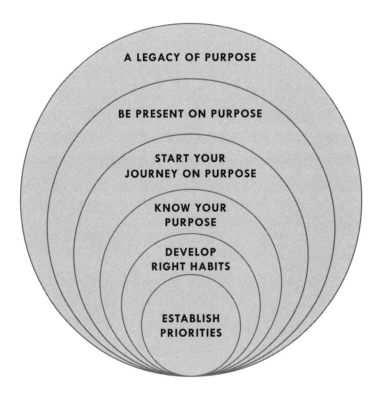

CHAPTER 1

A Foundation of Faith

I truly believe that if you don't choose your priorities, they will be chosen for you. Daily demands and incessant messages bombard us and vie for our attention. A fierce competition is constantly being waged not only for your time and money but also for your devotion. If not careful, you may find your affections and attention in default mode. You may be distracted by—or even fixated on—things that neither lead to your own best possible life nor improve your ability to create the best possible life for those you care about most. It is increasingly easy to be robbed of precious, finite time and energy that ought to be spent in pursuit of your own particular and unique purpose. You need to have clear, well-ordered priorities to help steer your decisions and inform your actions and pursuits.

As early as my teen years, I began considering what the primary focus of my life should be. Admittedly, my default priority at the time was to make me, myself, and I the top priority! It felt right to fully focus on my own wants and needs, especially on days when peers in school were hard to get along with or teachers, coaches, and even my parents seemed demanding and unfair. It was primarily hubris that led me to believe that I should be my number one priority. But it also seemed logical because, after all, if I didn't prioritize me, then who would?

Eventually, I came to believe that my tendency toward self-involvement and pride was a trap, lying in wait to steer me away from a more rewarding and fulfilling purpose that included using my gifts and experiences to serve not only myself, but others. But it was still a process to discover what my foundational priority should be.

Searching for Focus

Around late middle or early high school, I had decided that I wanted to get married and have a family of my own one day. I appreciated my parents and siblings and wanted to build on things I had learned growing up. I wanted to replicate some things and make other things better from my own upbringing. At the time, I didn't really have words for it, but I hoped to create an environment where each family member felt loved, encouraged, and valued. But having a family was a long way off, so it seemed that even family couldn't assume a top spot for my life priorities.

As a teen, I worked part-time mowing lawns to earn money. I was fortunate that I could earn money but didn't have to take on a full-time job yet. I loved playing sports, hanging out with friends, and doing other typical teenage fun stuff. Though I enjoyed these things, they would not necessarily serve me as a top focus in life long-term either. Most people don't go into professional sports, so I didn't want to center my life around that aim. I also figured that many of my friendships in high school would shift, as we pursued various pathways and assumed responsibilities. So I reasoned that neither family, friends, work, nor my favorite activities would serve as a foundational priority for my life.

At times, I might have been unusually focused on the future as a teenager! But after thinking through each of the previously mentioned aspects of my life and realizing that they may be ever-evolving, I found myself wanting a foundational priority that could serve as a bedrock—one that offered joy, assurance, and direction in navigating life's inevitable changes and challenges. I wanted a priority that was constant and reliable—one that would not change, even when circumstances and events changed around me.

A foundational life priority serves a function in our lives that is like the foundation of a house. If the foundation settles and cracks, it leaves the integrity of the whole house vulnerable. By the same token, even if some elements of a home's construction begin to falter, it can likely be repaired or renovated if the foundation is solid.

Putting Trust in God

I once visited the coastal town of Bar Harbor, Maine. I had never been to Maine, and I had heard about the beauty of this beach town with lots of lighthouses. I supposed that "Bar Harbor" got its name from the sailors and fishermen who needed a break, so they came and gathered at the bar after many hours spent at sea. That seemed plausible to this Midwesterner! It was, of course, incorrect. After arriving, I learned that the tides changed by many feet each day, influenced by the gravitational pull of the sun and moon, so the "bar" in "Bar Harbor" referred to the sand bars that appear at low tide and are covered when the tide rolls in. Everyone and everything on the shoreline responds to the shifting tides that happen every day. Boats must be careful when and where they tie up. Docks have stairs that are adjusted based on the tides. And of course, lighthouses warn boats of the hazards they need to navigate along the shoreline.

I had a chance to take a flight over the lighthouses in the bay. Many of them are hundreds of years old but are still in surprisingly good condition. Each one was constructed on solid ground or rock above the waves. Most people understandably focus on the powerful light emitted from lighthouses, since, of course, that is their primary function. But I was struck by the fact that lighthouses must be built with incredibly strong and durable foundations so that they can persevere through violent wind and storms, steadfastly providing their life-preserving light for the ships at sea. The foundation supports the lighthouse so it can fulfill its vital work and function in perilous conditions.

Similarly, a foundational priority in life holds together each of the other critical elements of our lives, even during hardships and storms, shaping our values and affording practical guidance that informs how we think and act. For me, it was clear that faith was the only priority that could meaningfully and capably serve as a foundation for each of the other priorities of my life. When the wind and waves of life come rolling in—and they do for us all—faith is the constant that cannot be shaken, providing light and hope for the present and the future.

Faith in God was the foundation that I needed and had been seeking. God existed before time. He is for us and provides truth and light in our lives. God's Son, Jesus, saves. His Spirit guides and helps—and I've sure needed a lot of it! God has also provided me with faithful, supportive friends along my journey, who have become like family.

God was here yesterday, is here today, and will be here for me tomorrow. He created me, the earth, and everything and everyone in it. I understand my unique purpose, and it is inextricably connected with His intent and design. I believe that God is the author and architect of my purpose and of yours. So I do not think it is possible for any of us to fully live out our purpose apart from Him. We all get to enjoy and experience this amazing earth with its diverse and complex ecosystems, and God intends for us to steward every corner of it well. I believe His intent is for us to make it a better place than it was before we arrived. We do that best when we discover and accomplish His purpose for our lives.

To make my faith in God my top priority, I knew that faith must not only be a stated value, rather, it must also be my top priority in reality and practice. I resolved that no matter what happened in life—through richer, poorer, sickness, health, highs, and lows—nothing would separate me from the love of God, as the Apostle Paul wrote in his letter to the church at Rome.[1] I aimed to love God, regardless of my circumstances. While I can never foretell or control all those circumstances, I can commit to holding fast to my faith in God. In turn, His promise is to never abandon me. I am determined to consult Him on my decisions and to respond and act based upon His answers, even when I don't like them. If faith in God is your foundational priority, as it is for me, then your direction and decisions start with Him. He has provided the help we need.

Laying a Foundation with Care

When I turned fourteen, I worked a summer job building concrete block foundations—a very tiring but rewarding job. Each day, regardless of how hot or cold the weather was, we started the day bright and early. I knew that it would be a tremendous workout hauling around thirty-eight-pound blocks and lifting them into place. I gained twenty pounds over that summer—mostly muscle—because of that physically demanding job.

---

1   Rom. 8:38 (New Living Translation).

I learned how critical it was to set the foundation correctly, and the most important job was the first step, when the foreman checked to ensure that the very first block was laid precisely straight and square. He got out the blueprint, found the lot pins, measured from the street, rechecked the lot pins, and measured again. We placed stakes in the ground and created a grid with string. Those strings had to be laid out perfectly for each corner of the property. It was critical to get this right because the rest of the house would, of course, be built on that foundation. Those foundational walls were designed to last for many, many years, if not forever!

Growing a foundation of faith looks a lot like laying a literal foundation. When you work to grow your spiritual life, you can experience a stronger and more robust faith. Like those precise measurements used to set that concrete foundation, God has established guidance for your life. He has given you an intricate framework to help you align your life with His intent and purposes, which are always designed for your good. The Bible provides insights into the ways we can live and serve each other, steer our futures, interact with our family and friends, manage and steward our finances, and engage at work. In studying a biblical framework for my faith, I discovered practical tips, songs of thanks and praise, prayers of hope, instructions for finding and being a friend, ways to address foes and avoid folly, and countless other principles to help steer my life. Additionally, there are countless stories of leaders, followers, and those learning how to lead and follow. These people were all working to figure out God's intent for their lives—with varying levels of success! Lots of these stories highlight cases of struggle and failures, but each narrative is a treasure trove of timeless wisdom and teaching that has helped grow an enduring foundation of faith in my life.

The beauty of life is that regardless of where you are, you can stop and start again! You can go as far as your humility will take you. You can create a more purposeful life irrespective of past choices or decisions you have made—or even consequences you might be living with—as long as you are willing to humble yourself and reprioritize your life. Today is the best day to start, and you start by determining your foundational priority. It is hard work to lay a firm and reliable foundation, and it might not be obvious to others at first what is happening to you. However, committing to making the shift will yield a more satisfying and fulfilling future for you.

You might think faith in God is not for you, and maybe you do not think you hear from God. But know that God's leadership in my life has convinced me that He also has a unique purpose for you. If you have wondered where God has been and looked for Him in your past, in your current circumstances, or around in your immediate environment, I'd suggest that you actively seek Him in the Bible. Try the Psalms and the book of John to start. You could begin serving others to help you reflect on and learn more about what He has uniquely gifted you to do. Or you might find a community of people who believe in and follow Jesus and ask questions of them. Importantly, that community connection doesn't have to happen on a Sunday morning at a church necessarily, though you certainly could start there. You will begin to feel His Spirit lead and nudge you toward His purpose for you. My hope is that you will find that, with the Bible and other believers to teach and guide you, faith can become your foundational priority in life.

I decided to let nothing usurp my foundational priority of faith—not success, failure, fun, or even tragedy. I had made the choice that no matter what comes my way, I would not abandon my foundation of faith. With that decided, I was prepared to consider my second priority: family.

CHAPTER 2

Framing a Focus on Family

Business empires and expansive faith-based institutions have been built in response to the understanding that family is important and rightly merits our focus and time. Such organizations exist in part because it can be a challenge to move from having good intentions to prioritize family to consistently *demonstrating* that family indeed is a high priority to you. I wrestle with this challenge and have implemented—albeit imperfectly at times—practices that help frame a proper commitment and focus on my family. It can be easy to state your family is a top priority, but too often people make excuses when it comes to following through.

I have been married to my wife, Dana, for twenty-five years, and we have four children—two girls, E1 and E2, and two boys, E3 and E4. (These are the nicknames we use when referring to them.) One of my chief aims as a dad is to create an environment that supports the discovery of their unique life purposes. I want to introduce them to opportunities that offer the best chance for them to explore, and ultimately discover, how and where they can apply and hone their interests, talents, and skills.

Dana and I have very different personalities, strengths, and even approaches to helping our children discover their purposes. That is a good thing, since, of course, our children have very different needs, personalities, gifts, and approaches to life's opportunities and daily stressors. Dana and I share the foundational priority of faith and a reliance on God, and we agree on certain immutable principles that steer our decision-making. We both want to teach our kids how to make wise decisions for themselves, learn to be good friends, and develop a vibrant faith. However, sometimes the approaches we bring to supporting our children are very different. Dana is compassionate and focused and firm when necessary, and she is always aware of their needs for a daily routine and the unusual, out-of-the-ordinary concerns. I tend to be more future focused with my direction and advice. Between us, we have both tactical and directional support for their daily and developmental needs and growth. It is a good balance, I think, in the ways we show and share our love and support.

Action versus Intention

If you want to frame up a clearer focus on your family, start by acknowledging your differences. I like, and will often recommend, formulas for many things in life to help manage time and energy and to create efficiencies to better focus on top priorities. But when it comes to focusing on your family in such a way that each member recognizes they are a real (and not just stated) priority in your life—that requires flexibility and responsiveness to their unique abilities and perspectives. I'm fortunate to have a life partner who helps to make that possible! If you do not have a committed life partner to lean on in this journey, find a space, such as a faith-based community, where you can invite someone to come alongside and support you with creating chances for your family members to discover their life purposes. I suggest that you even find someone who can offer a different approach from yours!

Of course, there are always stops and starts on the way as you steer your family members toward their own life purposes, but it's worth the investment of energy and time. If we can envision a positive, joy-filled future with, or even for, a family member who is struggling to do so, they may be more likely to embrace that future for themselves. Someone who knows their purpose experiences more fulfillment and joy, and that joy can be shared with others at home, work, and in the community. That sense of fulfillment is achieved because of deep engagement with—a passion and commitment to—the activity and the outcomes.

Consider the ways you spend your finite energy. Then, consider whether the ways you are spending that energy are improving or hindering the well-being of your family members. Assess whether your actions are having the effect you want them to have. In truth, it is impossible to invest energy, time, and attention just right 100 percent of the time, so give yourself a little grace as you figure it out.

Some choices are tougher than others when it comes to prioritizing family. However, those choices will become clearer if you create a picture of what you want to do with and for your family members. The oft-used cliches of "providing a better life" or "providing for my family's needs" are a starting point for framing a stronger focus on your family. You need to take steps to reorder your priorities and energy to ensure your family gets your best you more often.

I do frequent self-checks on my thoughts, words, and time to determine whether they align with my stated priorities of faith and family. I realized that one important way to help my children discover what brings them joy and fulfillment was to model that pursuit myself. I thought that it was important for my children to see me pursue my own purpose in life with joy, using my talents and interests, managing failures, and starting again to see that it was possible to honor my priorities as I pursue my purpose. I recently had a glimpse of the effect that living my life on purpose has been having on my children. I invited E2 and her friend to serve as photographers for our company's annual convention. They took photos of our award winners and honorees, my keynote addresses, and the other programming. It was such a privilege to have them both there to help document, and I really enjoyed seeing my daughter use her talent. Following the event, E2 wrote me a letter. She shared that she appreciated seeing ways that my work has an impact on people, their businesses, and relationships. It was a special moment to read that letter.

Besides modeling the pursuit of my own life purpose, I am intentional in helping each of my family members to discover and pursue theirs. It was my wife's purpose to invest her energies in our home and our children. Early in our marriage, it was not easy for us to arrange our finances for her to work at home full-time. She is enormously gifted at anticipating and meeting our children's needs, arranging their full lives as they became teens, and attending to the many additional details of managing our home. As they've grown older, she has also been intentional in reading Scripture and encouraged them to clarify and pursue their own foundations of faith.

As the partner who worked full-time, I had to be very intentional with the limited time I had to share with my family members each day. I was determined to carve out that time to spend with my children and help them discover their interests and unique purposes. When they were young, I biked a lot. A trailer on the back made it possible to be away from our everyday surroundings to take small excursions. During those rides, I reminded them that I loved them. I communicated principles and ideas that I hoped could benefit them for a lifetime. We talked about the beauty found in nature, the benefits of movement for good health, and virtues such as encouraging others or being truthful.

Prioritization in Practice

Like many parents, I have often wondered what things my children heard and understood from our conversations and how—or frankly, whether—they might apply them in their lives. But on occasion, we caught a glimpse of the ways those lessons were sinking into their minds and hearts. During one particularly long bike ride with my two daughters in Summit County, Colorado, I was huffing and puffing from exhaustion and was doubtful I'd make it up the final hill, pulling that trailer at altitude while carrying both of my girls. My oldest, E1, noticed my slow pace and wondered out loud why we were going so much slower and how much farther we had to go. Gasping for that elusive mountain air, I responded as cordially as I could muster, "Honey, I'm sure trying. But I am *really* tired." Without hesitation, she responded, "You can do it, Daddy! I believe in you!" That moment was a little peek into the care and encouragement that she readily shares with others. Today, she is a committed educator, leveraging her talent for remaining positive and encouraging, even when things are difficult, to help her students grow and learn.

Each of my four children enjoys sports, and my older son, E3, likes basketball in addition to other sports. I decided to volunteer to coach his basketball team for several years when he was growing up. I wanted to support him, but I also wanted to support his friends' development as well. It was a great opportunity to help my son and his teammates learn to manage the ups and downs that inevitably occur in sports, so they would possess some of the tools needed to navigate the inevitable ups and downs in life. Following one game, E3 was disappointed and discouraged because he felt he played poorly. I let him know the most important thing he could take away from that day was not his performance, but the ways he can progress next time. Every experience is a chance to learn more about how to improve, and absolutely no one will remember the specifics of your performance in a game you played as a kid.

My younger daughter, E2, is a creative, confident, independent thinker who enjoys making any room or space more interesting and inviting. She shares this talent and interest with her mom, who is very talented at helping spaces look and feel warm and hospitable. In her teens, my daughter decided to start a business using her love for making and creating things. When E1 was preparing to head off to college, she bought a banner to decorate her dorm-room wall. When it arrived, my wife told E2 she could have made one for her sister instead. Not long after that, Banners by E. was born! She chose her materials and began creating tailored, expressive banners for her customers. Her work graces the walls of dorm rooms around the country. I was careful to provide the support she needed, while letting her make creative decisions to keep her work progressing and her passion flourishing. To be sure, the way I coached my entrepreneurial daughter in her venture was different than the way I coached her brother in basketball, because they needed different things. E3 wants to act and finds it hard to wait, so I encouraged him to try things, to experiment and learn from what he tries, and then make decisions about what he wants to commit to do. My daughter, E2, wants to commit and see something all the way through at the outset, so I encouraged her to take a bit more time to decide—then choose and commit.

My youngest son, E4, is a tactile learner and enjoys fitting things together, building new things, and fixing broken things. He's always ready to hop into tasks that require experimenting with tools, and he relishes the challenge of solving problems. I have family members who have worked in construction, and I thought a building project would be a challenging, fun way for him to learn and practice some skills, and it was something we could do together. After kicking around some options, I decided we could build a tiny house. We didn't intend to *live* in the tiny house, but I wanted to explore the process of designing a functional, efficient space with my son.

I drew up the plans and shared them with the family. I ordered the trailer from a company in Colorado, ordered some instructional books, and watched plenty of YouTube videos. I brought the trailer to a nearby storage unit where we could build the tiny house, store the equipment, and work on it during our free time. I ordered wood and other supplies.

E4 was only about seven years old at the time, and he could not wait to hop in and help. He wanted to stay awake and work on that tiny house late into the night! He really loved using all the tools, hammering nails, or using a level to check the work. He also enjoyed designing and imagining how different aspects of the house could be built. He is always eager to share helpful advice with others. So, after we completed the house, we temporarily moved it into our driveway, and he hosted a sleepover with friends. He smiled ear to ear as he toured the neighbors. He loved explaining how he addressed tricky tasks and responded to questions from friends and grown-ups alike. It was easy to see how the experience had been a step in helping him to explore his purpose, using his affinity for building, as well as his ability to share stories and explain processes to others.

In addition to exploring and supporting their specific interests and skills, another way that I chose to invest high quality time with my children is by taking them each on a few adventures at twelve years old, fifteen years old, and following high school graduation. My intent was to take time out from daily demands, make some meaningful memories, practice asking and listening to their perspectives, and of course, offer age-appropriate guidance.

As each of my children turned twelve years old, I took them on a domestic trip in the US. They each chose where they wanted to go. For this first adventure, I primarily wanted to remind them how much their mom and I love and care about them and emphasize that we are committed to helping them make decisions that will benefit their long-term well-being and joy. We discussed that it might be challenging in the years ahead to understand why we permit some things but not other things. I tried to prepare them for a day when some of their friends may want to influence them to do things that don't align with our priorities and decisions. I expressed that our decisions would always be in the interest of their current and future best possible life. Each of these experiences was different and reflective of my children's individual interests and experiences. E3 is an adventurer, so we went white-water rafting. E1 prefers not to fly, so we did not go far. E2 feels most at peace in the outdoors, so we went to a scenic place to hike and take in new panoramic views. I am looking forward to the trip with E4 soon. Each adventure reflected their individual personalities and interests.

When each child turned fifteen years old, we joined a small team of volunteers for a short-term service project. It was important to Dana and me that our children develop compassion, empathy, a readiness to help, and a posture of gratitude rather than entitlement. We traveled to Ecuador and joined a local team of homebuilders. At the end of the trip, the kids wrote a brief note expressing their care and support for the new homeowners. They included a brief prayer in their best Spanish. It was a challenge, but meeting new people, volunteering their time and talents, partnering with others, and practicing a new language were experiences I hoped would serve them well throughout their lives.

Finally, following high school graduation, we traveled somewhere globally so that they could gain some experience in another culture. The intent was to expose them to the myriad opportunities available in the world for them so they could learn and grow. I also wanted to open their eyes to the vast diversity of human experience and to impress upon them the importance of demonstrating respect for all. I wanted to help them know that our experiences and perspectives are deeply influenced by our own environment and upbringing. I wanted to encourage them to connect with people who are different from them and help them know that listening well is one important step toward creating those connections. It was interesting to see the ways their personalities had shown through on their chosen excursions and to reflect on how much they had matured since our first trip at twelve years old.

Engaging at Home

It is a privilege to be able to travel and engage in projects and activities with my children. But the objectives of those adventures can be accomplished without big travel or construction projects included in the mix! I suspect that the daily interactions and moments spent reflecting on and underscoring key learnings and just having daily conversations had as much influence on my children's development as the getaways or activities themselves. Each moment with your family is a deposit you can draw on in challenging times and reflect on during times of celebration.

Start by picking a local spot to visit together to get a change of scenery and practice just hanging out! Be prepared to talk about likes and dislikes and, of course, be ready to share the values and principles that you want to instill. Pick a park, bring along a sack lunch, and commit to one conversation about what you want your family member to hear and know. Say the important words that describe what your family member means to you, how you feel about them, and what you hope for their future. Go ahead and pull out all the techniques you need to and treat your teenager to a favorite meal, and find time to chat for a few critical minutes, sans earbuds.

Additionally, while it is not possible for all families with young children to have a person who can commit to full-time parenting and working at home, consider ways you can maximize the valuable moments that you *do* have. Be intentional about meeting needs, differentiating needs from wants, and having conversations.

Stay inquisitive about what your family members need, think, and feel! There are many resources out there to help families make the most of their moments and relationships. Be proactive and seek them out.

Catalogue the most important topics, messages, and lessons you want to share with your family members. Commit to sharing one per week on the ride to school, during an impromptu video call, in a voice to text while commuting to work, on the bathroom mirror, or even in a postcard you drop in the mail.

Remind them that the world is big and so is their talent! Let them know that there are many opportunities to use their talent, accomplish good in the world, and fulfill their unique purpose. Your belief and hope for their future *will* make a difference!

The days sometimes feel long, especially for parents of young children. But during those longest days, remember that the years fly by at breakneck speed. With faith as a foundational priority, I find that it is easier to prioritize my family—even when those days feel long and hard.

Now is always a perfect time to reframe focus on your family, adjusting and applying your energy and time accordingly. Refuse to be the one who blinks and finds that time has passed and the messages and moments you had hoped to share along the way with your family members are no longer possible.

Do small things, starting today, that help frame a clearer focus on your family. Joy is shared and multiplied over time, as you invest in your family members' interests and hopes for the future. Even incremental investments of meaningful moments and conversations will provide a precious return over time that you—and they—will cherish.

CHAPTER 3

Created for Productivity

As a kid, I could never be still and always needed to be doing or thinking about something. I was rarely idle. I loved playing sports and through junior high I played basketball and football, ran track, and wrestled. In high school, I played football for a couple more seasons and wrestled all four years.

Like most kids, when I was young, I loved building forts. Unlike most kids, however, I liked building plans for my future, too. There were plenty of times when the four of us Nyffeler siblings got ourselves involved in mischief. Once, Mom bought a beautiful vase for the house—a new decorative item she adored. We were playing ball and, reminiscent of that once-famous *Brady Bunch* episode, one of us hit that vase, and it broke. "Mom always says, 'Don't play ball in the house,'" but we hadn't heeded her advice any better than the Brady brothers had. All four of us were immediately on the same team after that. We pieced that vase back together with the best glue we could find. It was years before Mom found out. More often than not, the outcomes of our shenanigans were evident, but the guilty parties were never quick to own up to it when things went wrong. My dad came to expect that whenever anything not good happened, it was obviously that mysterious fifth Nyffeler kid named "Not me!" who was forever the culprit.

It took a while for me to catch on to the fact that being busy and being productive aren't always the same thing. I think of productivity as an investment in time and energy in those activities that yield the most positive, hoped-for outcomes for yourself and others. While busyness also requires an investment of time and energy, some activities that fill our calendars may not always have the best outcomes. And of course, it is possible to be busy with things that result in negative outcomes, as my preceding story illustrates!

Applying Myself

As early as my teen years, I'd experienced enough negative consequences from my misdirected busyness that I made the decision to identify my life's priorities and planned to remain committed to them. I decided my third priority—behind faith and family—would be *productivity*, and I decided to expend my time and energy accordingly. Of course, I was still figuring out what it meant to be productive, rather than just *busy*, but I wanted my activities and effort to be purposeful and to result in the best outcomes. I filled my days with activities that would expand my learning experiences and develop new skills.

As I mentioned, I competed on the wrestling team in high school. It took a lot of my time during the season, but it was time well spent. I learned to manage discomfort and pain, to train hard through that discomfort, and to set and achieve goals. I learned to study and anticipate my opponents' strengths and weaknesses, as well as my own, and, like all athletes, I preferred winning over losing every day of the week. But it doesn't always go your way, so I also had to learn to express (at least a modicum of) sportsmanship in defeat. These were all valuable skills applicable in my life and work today.

Outside of high school wrestling season, I worked many different jobs. During the weeks that school was in session, I often worked twenty or more hours per week across two or three part-time jobs at a time. During holiday and summer breaks, I worked as many as sixty hours per week. I worked in a variety of industries and sectors, including telemarketing, construction, and restaurant jobs. Each one supported my learning and growth and showed me how to gauge productivity in different ways. It is regrettable that there's been a downward trend in the proportion of US teens participating in the workforce since their peak participation in the late 1970s. Fortunately, however, that trend appears to be reversing a bit in the wake of the global pandemic. When teens do not have chances for paid work, I think it is a missed opportunity to figure out what they like to do, practice what they do well, and gain valuable workplace insights that can serve them throughout their lives.

As a construction worker, I learned to be efficient with my energy because it was so physically taxing. One afternoon, I was about to walk up from a basement where our crew was laying a fresh foundation. My supervisor stopped me and asked where I was headed. I announced, "I'm walking up to my car to have lunch." With a sweep of his hand, he directed me to look around the basement. Pointing out the tools and equipment, he explained they all needed to make their way out of the basement, adding, "Never leave a space empty-handed because something always needs to go exactly where you are going!" It was a poignant and practical lesson in maximizing productivity and efficiency and using limited time and energy in the best ways.

I applied this learning in my jobs at various restaurants as well. At one location, I stocked the buffet at a local pizza place. I always remembered to carry items into the kitchen that needed to be cleaned or thrown away, and I never left the kitchen without bringing out a plate of food, condiments, or other items that needed to be served to guests. I noted the time it took for pizzas to bake, and even how long, on average, people needed to finish their meals. This allowed me to be responsive to customer needs and helped ensure that I served the freshest food. Again, I learned and practiced valuable skills in managing time, effort, products, and customer-service demands to create the best possible experience for guests.

As a telemarketer, one of my jobs was to entice people to change their long-distance carrier. It was my first role where performance metrics were directly tied to the role. Those metrics were continuously displayed on the computer in front of me. There were goals for the number of calls made, sales targets, and closing results. I enjoyed challenging myself to find ways to boost my productivity by focusing on the key words of the pitch and eliminating unnecessary words to communicate the key points more quickly. I practiced listening and responding succinctly to customers. I learned to type up the report for the call as I autodialed the next potential customer. I aimed to sell more with fewer dial-outs and to shorten the time it took to close.

Learning at Work

I had many jobs in my teens and early twenties, often three part-time gigs at once. I learned about sales, managing people and processes, customer service, policies, protocols, and how to ask and listen better. I worked for small- and medium-sized companies and, along the way, I figured out how to boost my productivity by studying, learning, and observing others and the ways they did their work. If I had idle time, I would find ways to work and learn and to learn at work. Many of those valuable lessons from my early jobs still inform my work habits and thought processes today. I seek ways to make conversations, meetings, tasks, and trips more efficient and productive, striving to create better experiences and outcomes for myself and those around me.

In high school, I also looked to maximize my learning and productivity, taking additional courses that were not necessarily required. I opted out of the study hall to take another class. One year I registered for three foreign languages—Spanish, German, and Japanese. By the time I completed my junior year in high school, I had accumulated a bunch of credit hours, and while my high-school grades didn't rival those of the top students, I was very curious. It was important to me to learn things that were applicable in my life and work, rather than only achieving certain marks or grades for their own sake. I particularly liked to observe others, their talent, ideas, and choices. Even as a teenager, I began to recognize how much our choices can influence our life trajectories.

Prioritizing productivity to the extent I have has a bit of a downside, I'll admit. As you might have deduced, I get bored easily and always need a new challenge or opportunity to capture my interest. My first semester in college, I feared that the experience would be a waste of my time more than it would enrich it. While I understood there was value in completing a degree, I didn't want to do it only because that was what others expected of me. I sought to craft a post-secondary education experience that had the most utility for my future.

I wanted to pursue a program that I could complete efficiently, and which had broad application, regardless of the industry or sector that I ultimately pursued. So I pivoted my degree from education to communications. One night, while sitting in my dorm room with the course catalogue open on the floor—yes, those printed paper manuals were still a thing when I was in college—I planned a pathway to degree completion, mapping out the next two-and-a-half years of classes. I told my parents that it was possible to complete my degree in three years if I took twenty-four credit hours, which I could do taking classes only on Tuesdays and Thursdays. That would free me up to work the other three days of the workweek. Then I could study and relax a bit on weekends.

My mom thought that was the least smart idea I'd ever had. She encouraged me to enjoy my college years because there would be plenty of time to work full-time for the rest of my life. But with productivity as one of my top priorities, I figured that I could be a better earner and employee in the long run if I worked smarter and, yes, a bit harder, to get my coursework done quickly while getting valuable work experience along the way.

Besides the well-intentioned pushback I received from Mom, I had another hurdle to get over in executing my plan: The university did not allow students to register for that many credit hours at one time. I had to petition the administration to let me do it. Apparently, no one had ever made such a request before, but I made my case. Administrators reviewed my transcript and grades up to that point and granted my request, but they clearly agreed with Mom and thought it was a nutty idea.

I had carefully plotted my coursework for each semester and grouped together courses that appeared to have some thematic or content overlap. I could think more thoroughly and deeply about specific topics, apply learnings immediately to another course, and build on each of my assignments and papers. One semester, I took nonverbal communications and an interviewing class at the same time. It was fascinating to think about the ways that nonverbal cues were important in understanding verbal feedback. I took a speech class the same semester I took a writing class and focused on similar topics and ideas. I was able to practice both speaking and writing on those topics, which accelerated my understanding of the content. My efforts felt more productive and efficient, as I leveraged learnings that helped me excel across courses.

Throughout my college years, I was able to practice being highly productive. I was very intentional with my time and energy, so when college was completed, I had accumulated a variety of experiences that I could build on to create a purposeful life. I stretched my entrepreneurial wings and had a business selling loft beds and then buying them back when students exited the dorms, only to resell them to the next student. It was a successful gig for a while. Typically, I balanced a full forty-hour workweek while continuing to honor my first priorities of faith and family. Sometimes I could produce more than some of my coworkers who spent more time working. I once had a successful run as a top seller of ad space for coupon books that were earmarked for students to increase traffic for local businesses. I practiced maximizing my time and effort and those new opportunities arose.

It was not my intent to simply stay busy or make more money in the moment. Rather, I wanted to create a track record of productively applying my time and energy. I engaged in activities that would prepare me to reap financial rewards later and that would also accelerate my ability to live a more sustainable and purposeful life each day.

I began practicing how to adjust my mindset toward productivity as a teen and a college student, and I still lean on those lessons today, long into my career and life journey. I tend to read multiple books at the same time on similar topics, for instance, so that I can have an internal conversation about the ideas between authors. I group my business meetings on similar subject matter, so I can make decisions that are aligned. It is rewarding to make the most of moments with the many people that I meet and work with, so like others, I schedule working lunches and even short walking meetings between calendared ones, so that I can have meaningful conversations along the way. The intent isn't to "fill up every waking moment" with a meeting, but, rather, to make the most of valuable moments that are available to ensure that my time at work is as productive as possible. This helps me to feel fully present when I'm focused on my top two priorities of faith and family.

Prioritizing productivity over busyness can lead to a more purposeful and satisfying life. Steering your focus toward productively applying your time and energy is very satisfying when your efforts yield more goodness and growth in your own life and in the lives of those you love and care about.

Start now to clarify your most important priorities. Do this *before* arranging and applying your time and effort. People sometimes get that out of order. Once you have determined your priorities, make decisions about how to use your time and energy most productively. Ensure that the allocation of your time and energy aligns with the stated order of your priorities. You will find that you have more capacity and energy than you realized when they are demonstrably earmarked toward things that are most important.

Busyness is too often used as a bulwark against doing the hard work of reflecting on what really matters most. Time fillers that do not support or yield the most positive, hoped-for results you want to see in your life can be a barrier to finding the best ways to spend your limited time and energy.

Whether you are just beginning your post-secondary education journey or you are years into your career, analyze the ways you are allocating your time and energy, and start making incremental changes that will allow you to steer your efforts toward greater productivity that aligns with your top priorities. The hours in your day *are* enough! You don't need more of them. Review the number of hours in your day and how your energy—not only your time—is spent. Consider the quality of that time and whether it is earmarked toward your biggest priorities. Question where you might reduce the time or energy it takes to complete a daily task, freeing that time to spend with a family member or a friend who is like family. Determine ways you can have meaningful conversations, complete tasks, and even partner with others to get work done.

Rest assured, you do not necessarily need to take twenty-four college credit hours to be more productive! But figure out what you most want to accomplish and what you most want to *learn*. Make and voice decisions about your priorities; share them with those you care most about, which can help cement your commitments and ensure that your vocation and work time do not usurp your other priorities. Then make subtle, or big, adjustments in your life and schedule to help make sure you are living your life more purposefully. And if you need to wait a while prior to making changes, soak up *all* the learning you can *right where you* are in the meantime. Shift your perspective and realize that every opportunity can lead to growth.

CHAPTER 4

Intentional Rest

People spend much time and energy trying to figure out how to enjoy life more. Possible hobbies and pastimes are fascinating to think about. They might include reading, writing stories, exercising, taking outdoor adventures, attending sporting events, socializing with friends or family at restaurants or entertainment venues, doing puzzles, or playing games online or in person. There are countless ways to spend our discretionary time resting and enjoying life. It is critical to make rest and enjoyment a high priority because, of course, our minds and bodies require rest to live healthy lives.

Occasionally, though, the highest priorities of faith, family, and productivity can be easily subverted by putting rest and enjoyment at the top. I've been tempted in my life to put fun ahead of my top priorities. I love to travel, and I enjoy spending quality time with my wife. I'd drop just about anything to do only these two things, so it can sometimes be tricky to maintain the right balance with my priorities in order.

As an example, I recently had a once-in-a-lifetime opportunity that challenged my commitment to my top priorities of faith, family, and productivity. A vendor of my business invited me to a multiday event related to the Super Bowl in Phoenix, Arizona. An array of festivities and parties was planned throughout the week. The timing of that invitation was a challenge to my stated priorities and commitment to keep my family and my faith first, mainly because I had been traveling nationally and internationally the previous couple of weeks and had additional travel planned for the week after. So, I felt stuck, trying to make a tough decision about whether to head directly to Phoenix for lots of fun around the big event, or honor my commitment to prioritize my family relationships ahead of my free time.

Everyone I talked to was telling me there was nothing to think about, noting it was an amazing one-time opportunity I shouldn't miss. But I was really wrestling with the decision because I had been away for a longer stretch than usual and needed to reconnect with my family. I felt that my commitment, even my character, was being tested, since I wanted my stated priorities to align with my decisions and actions.

As I inquired more about the week's agenda in Phoenix, I learned there would be events and parties late into the evenings with notable celebrities present. My colleagues expected me to lean into the festivities and enjoy the consecutive days of socializing. Finally, I decided to go, but I adjusted the expectations for my attendance and participation. I considered which events would leverage my time best for personal and professional connections and opted to attend some events, while forgoing the other activities, namely a golf outing and the late-night parties. (I usually score around seventy-two or so on a good day of golf, and then it tends to get worse on the back nine. So, skipping the golf outing wasn't that much of a sacrifice, it turns out!)

I decided to cut off one of my travel days, and Dana and I flew in late the next afternoon right before the first event. I am grateful that my wife could join, which was a big reason I decided to accept the invitation. It also happens that our two oldest children were students at a local university at the time, and we had the chance to meet up and share meals with them. It turns out that the experience really was a once-in-a-lifetime opportunity to enjoy time with my family while making some memories at the Super Bowl.

To enjoy your life on purpose, think more systematically and thoroughly about the priority of rest. Determine what will bring you the most short- and long-term joy and think about *why* those things evoke joy for you. This approach can help you to be more intentional and proactive with your choices in the moment. While the adventure in Super Bowl fun was an unusual and big event that ended up integrating well with my need to connect with my family, there are other smaller opportunities and daily decisions that can easily encroach on your time and threaten your relationships, if you are not paying attention. Leaning into fun and rest *at the expense* of other life priorities can later rob you of the joy and fulfillment you want to experience.

Mindfully Coordinating Downtime

My wife is very good at considering everyone's interests when coordinating family getaways. For example, I do not enjoy beaches at all. Even though my family likes beaches, I never feel relaxed when I'm there. I don't like the way sand gets everywhere and tends to stay around forever, wherever it lands. I dislike the taste of salt in the water and how the sand and salt dry out my way-too-sensitive skin. The water in the ocean is usually too cold to enjoy swimming much, and the traffic and limited parking at most beaches make travel frustrating. Nonetheless, a few of our family vacations have included warm climates with punctuated beach times to accommodate my other family members' preferences. I always bring along an umbrella and a good book, and scope out the best shops ahead of time, just to make sure I've got something to do while their skin gets dried out from sun and sand at the beach.

Don't stop at only assembling a mental—or actual—list of your favorite pastimes and hobbies. Consider *why* you enjoy certain activities, or why you don't. When you consider the reasons you enjoy your very valuable free time, it can help you steer that time more intentionally to maximize the joy it brings. For myself, I really enjoy competing. Running a half-marathon or lifting weights just to bulk up does not sound fun to me at all because I prefer competitive team sports and games like basketball and ping-pong. Yes, my heart rate jumps during epic ping-pong matches.

I appreciate that it may seem obvious, but it's worth noting that free time turns *not* fun quite quickly when you are with people who don't share your interests. So be intentional to carefully coordinate who you'll be spending your time with. As I mentioned, I enjoy traveling and seeing the world, and it's been a privilege to do that frequently. One of my favorite spots on the globe is New Zealand—not only because of its beautiful views and landscapes, but because the people are friendly and fun. I love anthropological questions and understanding the impact of the local environment on culture. I study the topography, elevation, proximity to water and transportation, and other things that influence the way people live and work there. I enjoy reading about the history of the government and political structures, infrastructure development, language, perceptions, religion, and other elements of the culture. I particularly love to study and process the ways that recent and historical leadership decisions have impacted the country and its people. While all of this is fascinating to me, it isn't for everyone.

I once took an overseas business trip with a coworker, and we had some rare downtime between meetings. We realized we had an opportunity to do some tourist activities, but it quickly became apparent that we did not share any of the same ideas about how to best spend that time. In the end, it was one of the least enjoyable trips ever for me, and it probably wasn't very fun for my colleague, either! It was a hard lesson that free time can feel like laborious, wasted time without good communication and coordination with the people you're spending it with.

Perhaps the most challenging, and probably the most important, logistical question to answer in making your plans for rest is *when* to schedule it. Find and schedule breaks and vacations when you can attend to the tasks that might cause you stress or worry if they pile up or must be urgently addressed when you return. My wife practices this judiciously. Before we leave on any trip, she wants a spotless, organized house, so we all do our best to chip in on that front. She spends hours picking up, doing laundry, paying bills, scheduling boarding for the dog, and many other tasks, so that when she is on vacation, she can enjoy it and know that she will return to order. It makes for hard work, but I appreciate her intentionality and the ways it frees her up to unwind when we are away.

I schedule a couple of short getaways with the family each year, as well as some time away with just my wife. We block out the dates and then determine where we would like to spend that time away. For our family, the week between Christmas and New Year's Day works best for our respective calendars, and it happens to be a time that is a bit slower at work. For you, it may be a different time of year, depending upon school, work, or other personal calendars. But don't wait. Schedule a quick time to get away, relax, and reconnect. It is about the time away and the time together. It is much less important where that is. A staycation can also be a brilliant way to enjoy your own town or region and make some meaningful memories with those you care about the most.

Being more intentional with scheduling your rest will be a boon to your life and well-being. Consider *what* to do with your free time, *why* you enjoy different activities, *who* you want to spend that time with, and *when* it will bring the most refreshment to you and others who join you. Pausing to reflect on these questions more intentionally will help you to make the most of those critical times of rest, relaxation, and recuperation.

Reflecting on Rest

A favorite passage of mine from the biblical creation story is a big moment when God pauses to consider all He has made and saw that it was "very good!"[2] This translated version of the ancient Hebrew text includes an exclamation point to help underscore the delight and abundance that are evident in God's creative work. In subsequent verses, the scripture says God blessed the seventh day and rested. Even a highly productive God, who does not need rest in the sense of recovering from all His hard work, paused to enjoy it, and rested *in* it. In this, God models for us how to pause, bless, and reflect on the created order, which was truly good.

Importantly, opportunities for rest and relaxation should not only be scheduled a couple of times per year. Your days and weeks should be punctuated with intentional pauses and rest time, so that you can experience a mental break and reflect on what you have accomplished. If you have flexibility to adjust your break times during the day, consider your daily energy levels to inform you when to break for lunch, for example. I leave the office each day at lunchtime to get a mental and physical break and try to eat a meal that will give me energy throughout the afternoon. This works best for me, and my first afternoon appointment is typically at one. Again, if your work affords you that opportunity, plan your breaks when you most need them to rejuvenate.

---

2   Gen. 1:31 (New Living Translation).

Review your calendar for the year and coordinate proactively with those you want to spend your rest and vacation time with. Don't delay. Consider your project load, deadlines, critical meetings, and personal obligations as you schedule your downtime. Take time away when you have the best chance of maximizing your rest and recuperation. Look at *when* you will need or most benefit from a break. Look at *why* you would enjoy a particular activity, and then plan to spend it with family or others who will most enjoy that time with you. Prioritize and protect that valuable, limited rest time with the same fervor you would your other important obligations.

Keeping your priorities well-balanced is about sharing your time in intentional and disciplined ways to ensure that you can be your best self for those who need you most. Scheduling time for rest and enjoyment will help with decision-making, ensure you have needed respite and recuperation, and can support you in living a more purposeful life. Wrestle with and pursue your faith, invest quality time making memories and growing with your family members, be productive in your vocation and other pursuits, and then adopt a cadence of enjoying and reflecting on your creativity and productivity. Build in meaningful rest and enjoyment that leads you to bless—express happiness with and for—those things that you've created, labored over, and shared with others.

Develop Right Habits

We all build the elements that make up our lives around our thoughts. Thoughts are translated to words, and words influence actions. Actions can be practiced repetitively, and if you practice often enough, while you'll certainly improve, you are also sure to encounter resistance and obstacles on your journey to fulfilling your purpose. Those obstacles can be the most important teacher. They can teach you perseverance. Those are the times you learn the most about yourself and your potential. If you develop the right habits, they will enable you to attend well to each of your life's priorities.

CHAPTER 5

Think Well

It has been said that if you want to know where a person is headed, look at their habits. I think this is largely true. I would add that if you want to understand their habits, know their thoughts. One of my favorite pastimes is watching championship sports of any kind. I love watching athletes compete at the highest level for something they have wanted and trained for their entire lives. In a championship setting, they are at that long-awaited moment when their lifelong goal could be reached within mere minutes or hours. The main reason I enjoy watching this highest level of competition is because of how much the athletes' mental state influences their performance and outcome. The game is all about their thoughts.

Most athletes competing at the highest level of their sports have trained for decades. There may be some differences in their physical attributes, but overall, those are relatively negligible. They have all received elite coaching, training, and nutrition, so on championship day, these are not the things that will decidedly move the needle in one direction or another with respect to the outcome.

The difference-maker on championship day is *mindset*. What matters most is thought life. Arnold Palmer rightly noted, "Success in this game depends less on strength of body than strength of mind and character."[3] And when that mindset is rooted in confidence, the opportunity for success is much greater. What matters is what they believe about themselves; what they know and understand about their opponent; what they plan to do; and then, how they execute their plan. In the seminal moments of the competition, after pushing their minds and bodies to the limit, they must fight off the nagging temptation to entertain self-doubt, which can undermine their efforts and sabotage their success. Champions must believe so strongly in their ability that there is simply no room for anything else—no room for worst-case scenarios and no room for fear.

Cultivating Confidence

Like elite athletes, it is important for you to reflect on what you believe about yourself. The onslaught of messages from social media, for example, can condition you to incessantly compare your life to others'. The standards conveyed by these mediums may be unrealistic and unattainable—for beauty, happiness, notoriety, or fame. Researchers warn that comparing yourself with others, especially in a world where technology is leveraged to perfect the plethora of images and words that bombard your feed, can breed negative, even destructive, self-talk.[4]

---

3   "Golf Legend," Arnold Palmer, accessed June 5, 2024, https://www.arnoldpalmer.com/golf.

4   "How Social Media Can Negatively Affect Your Child," Health Essentials, Cleveland Clinic, January 15, 2024, https://health.clevelandclinic.org/dangers-of-social-media-for-youth.

Instead of fixating on the standards set by others and comparing yourself to them, focus on aspects of your life that you can improve, such as growing in confidence or courage, expressing care for others, deepening friendships, developing new skills, or any number of things you could focus on. You will never become someone else, but you can become a better you tomorrow than you are today. Focus much more of your time and effort on developing the future self you want to become than you spend worrying about others' perceptions of your present self. This simple shift in your mindset and perspective is an important first step in living a life that is more fulfilling and purposeful.

It may take a while for that mindset shift to stick, so give yourself some time to practice thinking better thoughts. From there, as Shane Lopez describes in his book *Making Hope Happen*, you begin to build on the belief that your life can be even better tomorrow than it is today. Then begin to think about objectives you have for each of your top priorities. Be succinct as you consider the actual or imagined barriers and challenges you might need to navigate to realize progress on those objectives. Next, work backward from your objective, breaking down, step-by-step, what is required to get to that aspirational future state and ultimately win your own personal championship. Each of these steps begins with your thoughts rather than your actions. Thinking, then planning, can help you make sense of what you really mean to accomplish.

In addition to identifying each step, consider carefully how to accomplish each one. Contemplate, especially, what the very first step really is, as we sometimes inadvertently skip over the actual starting point. Also consider how you will gauge your progress in attaining your objective. As a superstar athlete thinks and prepares relentlessly for their championship moment, you, too, can be more intentional with each thought and step so that you are more focused on your priorities and objectives, making every moment more purposeful.

For me, producing this book is an exercise in staring down self-doubt. For years, different people have suggested I write a book, but self-doubt prevented me from launching into it. I had plenty of negative messages running through my mind: No one will read it, I'm not sure I have anything worthwhile to say, I don't have time to do it, or writing is not my gift. At some point, I determined to put the doubts and negative messages to rest and focus my thoughts on ways I could get the task accomplished. I applied the preceding framework, changing my thoughts, thinking about what outcomes I hoped to achieve, and carefully considering the steps needed to get a book written and produced.

As a father of four and a business owner, finding time to write is a definite challenge, but I reasoned I could allocate one hour per evening to writing the book, rather than watching a show on TV. I needed a framework for the content, so I outlined the sections and chapters for *Transform through Purpose* that reflect the things I believe and have aspired to apply in my life. I took some time to research what it takes to write and produce a book and leveraged insights I'd gained from reading hundreds of authors and titles to inform my content and process. When I had arrived at the seminal moment of the project and was on the precipice of completing my first book, my focus intensified on the finish line to prevent my self-doubt from thwarting the outcome. It is now finally completed.

Defeating Self-Doubt

Seeds of self-doubt are indeed like the weeds that try to take root in flower beds each spring. They will take a mile if given an inch. So how do you combat that persistent self-doubt to keep it from spiraling out of control? Start with realistic thoughts about yourself. I realized very quickly in my athletic career, for example, that becoming a professional athlete was not a reasonable aspiration for myself. While my effort was always high, I do not have the talent and capacity needed to achieve the highest level in sport. Be honest with yourself about where your strengths and abilities lie. Your capacity for success is multiplied when you understand and build on those abilities.

It is true and realistic for you to be better tomorrow in some way than you are today. The key is focusing your effort on the places where you have the most potential for growth and success—where you have the most capacity to shine. Believe that you have abilities you can use to achieve your objectives. Name and catalogue them. They are some of the best internal tools to help you realize your best future and fulfill your purpose.

Self-doubt can be defeated in your life, so it does not hijack your pursuits. If you're reading this today, that alone is evidence that it is possible to change your thoughts. Refuse space for self-doubt. Think well and directionally toward the next step of your plan to help you progress, so that you, too, can experience a personal championship in your life.

CHAPTER 6

Clearly Crafted Words

Once your thoughts are rightly focused, you can take the next step in building strong habits by crafting words, which serve to clarify and solidify your intent. When you put words to your thoughts and share them with the right people, it can provide some helpful accountability and invites others to support those intentions.

Early in my life, I began putting words to my thoughts—statements that clarify and drive my actions. My wife once joked, "Reed, you know the problem with your dreams? They become reality!" My thoughts are translated to carefully crafted words, which in turn drive the actions that I take.

I was eighteen years old when I first recall translating a big idea into words. I made a proclamation that took me many years to realize. I was hanging out with one of my best friends, and he told me that he had to leave. When I asked where he was going, he said he was headed home to see his sister who had just returned home from college. I didn't even know that he had a sister. (Yes, he really was a good friend of mine. But obviously my skills of observation and perception were not so well developed at that age.)

My friend asked if I wanted to come along. I was smart enough to say "yes" to the invitation, and that day I met the most amazing person— Dana. After meeting her, I immediately wondered how I would break the news to my friend that I was interested in dating his sister. Those who know me will not be surprised that I didn't wait very long.

Over the next couple of days, I planned out how I would talk with my friend about asking his sister out on a date. When I finally brought it up, he said, "Well, if any of my friends were to date my sister, I guess you're the best choice." I was glad for the vote of confidence, and I invited Dana out on our first date. I was sure glad when she agreed. When I met her, my first impression was that Dana was (and is) an incredible person. Our first date confirmed it.

My friend asked how the date went, and this was the first time I can remember translating a big thought into words that would take some years to come to fruition. I replied, "I think I am going to marry your sister." He told me he didn't think I should tell her that. That was probably good advice. Over the next three years, 1,500 miles separated us during college. I was attending the University of Nebraska in Lincoln, and Dana was in Alabama at Samford University. She broke up with me a few times along the way, as we navigated the distance and my need to mature, but finally, three-and-a-half years later, we were married. And of course, she is one of my greatest gifts! She's smart, caring, and loving. She was studying to be an educator, and she wanted to use her learnings as a stay-at-home mom to teach and care for our children. She is patient and supportive of decisions with my career that not only impact my life, but hers as well. Even when there were obstacles challenging our relationship, I did not lose sight of my vision and hope for the future.

Meeting Dana and thinking about our possible future life together was refining and affirming. I worked hard on my communication, worked to learn the things I needed to do to be a good friend and partner. I was determined to always honor my word and follow through, so she knew that what I said was true and reliable, and I learned to be a better encourager. Over time, Dana came to know that she could trust my words because I followed through with the things I promised. I am very grateful for our life together.

Watch Your Words

Consider, again, your own thoughts. What do you believe about yourself? Do your words reflect those thoughts? Do your words drive you to the right kinds of action, or do they prevent you from making progress toward your more purposeful life? Evaluate your thoughts, then work on crafting statements and refining your language so it can help propel your actions and lead you another step closer to a more purposeful life.

When things are difficult and you experience obstacles or barriers along the way, revisit your intent and the words you stated to clarify your positive future vision. Practice unwavering hopefulness that your goals can become reality. Dr. Martin Luther King Jr. brilliantly and passionately crafted words to paint a verbal picture of his dream: a community marked by freedom and equality for all. In sharing his vision, he helped steer and propel a multigenerational movement. When powerful words are born from right thoughts that first originate in quiet, they can become a critical component of driving positive change.

Think about who you want to be and what it will take to get there. Then tell others what you are going to do. Recent research by Howard

Klein at The Ohio State University's Fisher College of Business suggests that sharing your goals with someone whose opinion you respect can positively influence your journey to achieving your goals.[5] This will help spur you to action and ensure your progress—even incrementally—toward a more purposeful life.

5   Jeff Grabmeier, "Share Your Goals—but Be Careful Whom You Tell," Ohio State University, *ScienceDaily*, September 3, 2019, https://www.sciencedaily.com/releases/2019/09/190903084051.htm.

CHAPTER 7

Action!

One of my favorite sayings is "information without application is worthless." People often want to understand others' thoughts, words, or intent. However, the words have true power only when the listener has a response. The power comes to light when there is action. Words are often designed to influence action—or reaction—but of course that does not always happen. This is true for our own thoughts and words as well. Changing your thoughts and mindset, and even changing your words and language to align with those right thoughts, yields results only when those thoughts and words move us to action.

I've studied the lives of historical figures, people from the Bible, and contemporary leaders. I'm curious about what things led to their positions of leadership and what made them successful. Some of them have backstories that do not seem much different from what most of us experience. When you learn about their families, childhoods, or where they were raised, there is often not anything notably unique.

However, one thing that seems to stand out in reading about their lives is that, often times, between the ages of ten and twenty years old, they had a significant shift in mindset. They began to believe that impossible things were possible and to believe that they could make a difference. This is true for Abraham Lincoln, Martin Luther King Jr., Condoleezza Rice, Steve Jobs, and others. After this turning point, they began to communicate their ideas and plans, sharing them with colleagues or friends.

Growing up in a racist and segregated society, Martin Luther King Jr. began to socialize his ideas on establishing equality for all early in his life. As a trained Baptist minister, he spoke and wrote about them at innumerable events and spaces. In 1959, he spent some time with Mahatma Gandhi and a few of his close followers and relatives. Dr. King was influenced by Gandhi's commitment to equality and justice and his nonviolent approach. Dr. King's messages resonated deeply and widely, and participation in nonviolent protests helped to further accelerate the civil rights movement. His powerful words and actions resulted in critical changes. Although he faced racism, oppression, and violence and was tragically assassinated for standing up for his beliefs, our world is better today because of Martin Luther King Jr.'s decisions to speak and act.

From Words to Deeds

Leaders establish their thoughts and intent, and clarify their resolve, as they speak about and describe their ideas. They begin to see results as they start to act, taking that first step toward making those ideas reality. They say "yes" to the journey, even without knowing what will come their way. Stories that focus on this moment are powerful. Some favorite movie scenes, for example, include a moment when the hero says "yes" to the journey, not knowing where it will take them, but their resolve compels them to act. In Joseph Campbell's seventeen (later twelve) steps of the hero's journey, there is a moment when the hero crosses the threshold. They act, leaving the relative safety of their lives, accepting the journey, regardless of what it will entail. Whether it is Neo taking the red pill in *The Matrix*, Luke Skywalker deciding to save Princess Leia, or Katniss Everdeen volunteering as tribute, these are pivotal moments because the one who acts inspires a revolution.

Regardless of how strongly you believe in your ability or how articulately you state your intent for the future, your life will only change when you *act*. You must proceed in deed. Take a first step toward your stated objective, even if you think you will stumble or experience resistance. Objectives are reached through action.

Taking the first step is usually hard. It's like watching a baby wobble as they take those first steps. You may feel unsure and unstable. It will be difficult to change your habits, but once your thoughts and words are set in the right direction, you can act even if doubt, resistance, or constraints attempt to get in the way. You may need to make sacrifices that are uncomfortable or even scary, which is why your mindset and directional thoughts must remain steadfast. This was the case for many leaders I've enjoyed reading about. The resolve they established at an early age was so deeply ingrained that they created a kind of reality distortion field to protect their ideas, such that everywhere they went and whatever they experienced, their belief in their ideas and objectives never wavered.

If you want to experience a revolution of your own, or even a meaningful *evolution*, you must stand strong and hold fast to your ideas against resistance. You may have (internal or external) voices telling you that you're not capable, you may experience financial setbacks or other unexpected personal costs, but if your thoughts are right, your words are clarifying, and you take one step with the intent to change, these actual and perceived obstacles can serve to refine—not dismantle—your resolve. Lean into your resolve and take a second step.

It will build your confidence, reinforce your right thoughts, and build momentum for your actions. Actions are where meaningful change begins to take shape.

CHAPTER 8

Practice Diligently

A commitment to practice is imperative if you want to approach perfection in any endeavor. Perfection lies on the other side of practice. It is not enough to take just one step or complete one repetition. In a society that has grown accustomed to quick service, quick responses, and quick rewards, it can be difficult to accept that it may take many tries and many years to begin to see a return on your efforts.

In *Outliers: The Story of Success*, Malcolm Gladwell popularized the assertion that it takes 10,000 hours of practice to approach greatness at something. While the amount of time likely varies depending upon the task and arena, those we admire have undoubtedly practiced for years before they achieved the imagined greatness. Caitlin Clark spent years developing her skills as a young basketball player in Des Moines, Iowa, even playing on boys' teams in her youth, before she changed the trajectory of women's basketball during her four years at the University of Iowa. Her college years provided the stage for her to showcase skills she'd been developing over the previous decade. She reset the bar on excellence, leaving a cache of newly established collegiate records in her wake. And she hasn't even turned pro yet as of this writing. Before formally entering politics, Ronald Reagan spent years refining his views surrounding individual freedom and government in what is referred to as "The Speech." Thomas Edison and his team of researchers famously conducted thousands of experiments in their work to perfect a long-burning electric light bulb with a filament that would not quickly combust. And Yo-Yo Ma, a prodigy who began to focus on cello at the tender age of four, came to promote thinking critically about practice as a primary means for achieving excellence on any instrument. So, while it's clear the amount you practice is critical, how you *spend* that time is also important.

When athletes, artists, entertainers, professionals, and research-ers realize extraordinary levels of achievement after many intentional hours of practice, it inspires awe in those of us who watch. So don't undervalue the role that practice plays in creating habits that can set you on a strong course for fulfilling your purpose. To create the right habits, first generate right thoughts and clarifying words, then act, and practice every step.

Like lots of kids, I did not like homework at all. I thought school was a waste of my time and that the assignments were busywork. I thought teachers didn't really know what they were doing nor did they under-stand what I needed. Homework felt like a barrier to doing the things I most wanted to do. I really didn't understand the value of practice in school. But as I began my professional life, I started to appreciate the importance of practice. When I didn't practice well, I had a much lower ceiling for success. It was clear that I needed to sharpen my tools, so I started to break down each of the things I wanted and needed to work on to be more effective as a communicator, a leader, and a visionary. Then

I determined my aspirations for these areas and began to take steps to operate at a high level for each.

Getting Better, Step by Step

Talented leaders, it has been documented,[6] have many unique characteristics. They are visionaries who communicate openly, who demonstrate courage and act, and who have high ethics and empathy. The leaders I studied were always persistent and resolved, even in the face of hardship or resistance. Regardless of what they encountered, they were indefatigable. These were things I hoped to improve and thought would be worth my time and effort as I grew and pursued my own purpose in life.

I wanted to develop these traits and create habits around them. I began to practice—allocating time during my week to practice and get better at these things—about thirty minutes each day. In the same way that some people will train physically, I trained my thinking and other skills. For example, I practiced storytelling and speeches, focusing on nonverbal communication, inflection, and pacing. I practiced scenario thinking and worked through ways I would advise colleagues and other leaders.

I needed to break down my practice process in a stepwise manner. I liken my work here to practicing basketball. One year, I was coaching E3's basketball team. I had the kids shoot free throws to close out practice. Each athlete was different—height, strengths, and techniques—and it seemed the corrections they needed individually were limitless. Our shots from the line were inconsistent, not only from player to player, but from game to game. I decided to invite my very

---

6   Sunnie Giles, "The Most Important Leadership Competencies, According to Leaders Around the World," *Harvard Business Review*, March 15, 2016, https://hbr.org/2016/03/the-most-important-leadership-competencies-according-to-leaders-around-the-world. See also: James R. Detret, *Choosing Courage: The Everyday Guide to Being Brave at Work* (Cambridge, MA: Harvard Business Review Press, 2021).

skilled brother-in-law to coach up our team's free-throw shooting. In his senior year at the University of Nebraska-Lincoln, he was a talented long-range shooter, hitting more than half of his three-point shots and setting a school and Big 12 record.

He broke down the process of shooting a free throw into specific steps for the kids. He started with positioning their toes and feet. He explained how their thighs and hips should align with their shoulders and instructed them on the position and form for their arms, hands, and fingers. He then worked on their head position and focusing their eyes until finally he had them shoot free throws. Interestingly, his instruction wasn't on making a basket, and he didn't focus much on the hoop at all in these initial drills. He focused on the little steps they should take to boost the possibility that they could shoot the basketball correctly, so it had a better chance at going in the hoop.

Your practice, too, can fail for the same reason the kids missed all of their free-throw shots in the early season. They were focused on the outcome of making the basket and simply getting the ball in the hole by any means necessary. But they didn't understand the little things that they needed to do to achieve that outcome. Practice sometimes fails to yield the desired results. The kids who missed all their shots were focused on the goal—making the basket—not on what they needed to do to get better, step by step.

I applied this reality to my own efforts to improve in a few leadership areas. I steered my focus toward getting better at the little things. One of my early career goals was to improve my ability to influence others in a positive way. There were a few times I had some influence over those under my leadership. For instance, when I was the captain of the wrestling team my senior year, people would follow my lead because they were held accountable by the coach if they didn't. However, as a student walking the halls of the high school outside of that context, I had no influence.

I studied why people listen and act in response to one leader versus another. I learned that one important element is that leaders learn to communicate messages about decisions and ideas that are beneficial for the follower. I needed to figure out how to communicate messages that helped my potential followers understand how decisions could benefit them and the ways in which hoped-for outcomes were mutually beneficial.

When I realized this, I began to break down the conversations, starting with the greeting. The greeting would connect us and be designed to establish trust. I could learn about the person and find common interests to build trust. I studied popular conversation topics and became appropriately conversational in those topics that most appealed to a broad audience. In one recent conversation with an existing partner, we met in person for the first time. I enjoyed making an initial connection and learned about how they started their business. Some trust had already been established due to existing work and partnership, but I quickly recognized an immediate connection for the next phase and opportunity. Years of practice with these kinds of connections helped to make this conversation exciting and beneficial for us both.

Practicing Influence

While I worked a good deal on what I thought could be the right things to say, I worked even harder on active listening. I began by asking open-ended questions to provide a chance for them to share a story. I shared back a few points that I heard and prompted a few follow-up questions. I worked on my nonverbal communication elements, including my tone, pace of speaking, body language, my vocabulary—taking care to use vernacular that suited the audience, as well as eye contact and other elements to help level up my communication in hopes of improving my capacity to influence others.

I got better at it over time due to much practice, and I recently had a chance to have another important conversation. Recently, our company began to partner with a fast-growing startup with an energetic, talented founder. She mentioned in a conversation that she needed partners and felt pressured to take them on. I asked if she'd be willing to meet about that. She agreed. I suggested that sometimes we feel a need to take on partners because there is a gap or barrier that we feel is real, but that might not be as acute a challenge as we perceive it to be. In other words, the barrier is often more self-imposed than it is real. She called me later to say she'd paused, prayed, and ultimately, agreed it wasn't the right partnership. She explained to the potential partners that she was not ready for their investment. She received a great deal of aggressive push-back, which didn't cause her to waver in her decision. Rather, it helped to confirm her decision. She now feels more aligned with her customers, her employees, and the future she envisions for the business. It was clear the potential partners were in the deal only for their own benefit, which is not how she wants to build the business.

Practice takes time, and using your gifts and your purpose to support others requires—and is worthy of—your diligence. I focused on different aspects of speaking and leadership skills at different times to leverage those in accomplishing my purpose. Just like the kids worked on specific elements of shooting free throws, I focused on different elements of influential communications and practiced as often as I could.

Start by working on right thoughts, then clarify your thoughts through words, determine your first step to act—then practice, practice, practice! You are on your way to developing strong habits that will serve you well in pursuing your life on purpose.

CHAPTER 9

Persevere from Here

Children are naturally curious. They move into places and spaces to explore things they want to touch, feel, and experience. Early childhood educators are experts at providing safe, engaging ways for young children to learn about their environment. As humans grow, we read and study to learn more on topics that interest us. When we enjoy an activity, we focus on how to get better and improve our performance. But sometimes, that natural curiosity and interest wanes. Maybe our curiosity is satisfied, or monotony takes over our minds, making us feel a need to switch things up. Disinterest sneaks in, or maybe a disaster ensues, and we stop our pursuits. However, when it comes to pursuing your purpose, you ought to never be burned out or bored. Instead, it should ground you and propel you forward in a way that, regardless of the circumstances, you stay motivated to pursue it. Perseverance itself takes practice and is the point at which your habits are most tested but also rewarded.

Your purpose underlies all of what you do. Whether you change locations or vocations, friendships evolve, or your interests shift, your purpose should endure throughout your life. If your purpose is to build or create things that bring safety, joy, or enhance the community, there are innumerable ways you can fulfill your purpose. If your purpose is to help, heal, or encourage others, there are many places, spaces, and activities where you can pursue that lifelong purpose. And even when difficult roadblocks and heartaches in life arise, your purpose serves to propel you forward, albeit sometimes via a different road. Leaders that live in consistent pursuit of their purpose until the day that they die can create a legacy that ripples through time.

Optimism in the Face of Adversity

At a time when my business was growing quickly, we needed capital. I had already invested all my resources and assets, even sold my car, to help keep us afloat. I had an investor who was willing to come in at that moment, but I knew that it wasn't the right kind of partnership. It was a tough decision to turn it down and wait for the right opportunity. That next six-to-nine months was very difficult, with the business and well-being of many people hanging in the balance. Finally, the right partner came along, and we were able to structure the partnership in the best way. It was such a stressful time that required a great deal of faith and perseverance to get through.

Legacies are built amid perseverance through hardship. When you persevere in pursuing your purpose relentlessly, you model for others that not only is it possible to move forward, but it is also worth it. You may get exhausted, busy, bored, or distressed when difficult obstacles, emotions, and circumstances arise and threaten to derail you. But it is in those moments that perseverance comes into play, and legacies are born.

Jerry Rice is a legendary NFL receiver who played fifteen seasons for the San Francisco 49ers and five more with other franchises to conclude an impressive twenty-season career. Rice was known for his incredible work ethic. In his book *Talent Is Overrated*, Geoff Colvin says Rice was particularly known for his "six-days-a-week offseason workouts, which he conducted entirely on his own." He noted, when "players would sometimes join Rice just to see what it was like . . . some of them got sick before the day was over." Rice trained for hours on end to become an elite athlete, and he was extremely diligent about the quality of his effort. Rice pushed past initial perceived limits, persevering through much pain to improve his strength, speed, and agility. He left an enduring legacy in the league and was inducted into the Pro Football Hall of Fame in 2010, holding the NFL record for receptions.

There are tools researchers have found that enable humans to persevere in very difficult circumstances. A longitudinal study of prisoners of the Vietnam War was published in 2012.[7] Results indicate that optimism predicts resilience among repatriated POWs. Segovia et al. concluded that optimism, among several variables tested (e.g., officer/enlisted status, age at captivity, length of captivity, and so on), was the most significant "protective factor for confronting trauma." Researchers also suggest the possibility for providing "training to increase it."

There can often be very poor mental and physical outcomes due to exposure to extreme stressors like maltreatment, torture, and isolation. However, optimism—the tendency to have positive expectations of the future—serves as a buffer during such adversity. In his book *Good to Great*, Jim Collins explores the concept of the Stockdale Paradox, which describes some elements that enabled Admiral James Stockdale to endure

---

7   Francine Segovia et al., "Optimism Predicts Resilience in Repatriated Prisoners of War: A 37-Year Longitudinal Study," *Journal of Traumatic Stress* 52, no. 3 (June 2012): 330–336, https://doi.org/10.1002/jts.21691.

brutal captivity during the Vietnam War, while also supporting his fellow prisoners. He maintained an optimistic outlook and demonstrated resilience that also accounted for the reality of his current circumstances. While he maintained a belief in the possibility of rescue at some point, he did so while realistically examining the current and potential future state for himself and others. He developed methods and rules for coping with the pain and hardships in the interim, such as setting small goals to endure trauma for a few short minutes, then reassessing. Stockdale's experience and perspective suggest that proactively maintaining optimism is not the same as what some refer to as "blind optimism." In other words, optimism is not equivalent to simply *wishing* for something to happen while ignoring the bad stuff. This approach can feel crushing when the expected outcome does not happen because you have no means of coping with that failed future in the moment. Optimism, instead, involves maintaining a mindset that acknowledges the current reality, and involves employing tactics that enable perseverance through the current hardships, which in turn maximizes the chance for a better tomorrow.

Ernest Shackleton led an expedition from London with the intent to traverse the continent of Antarctica. The team set sail on the ship *Endurance*, but the journey was thwarted when, in 1915, it became trapped in ice in the Weddell Sea. After many months of drifting with the ice pack, the crew abandoned the ship and took precarious refuge on Elephant Island. The ship eventually sank to the bottom of the sea. Shackleton; Frank Worsley, the ship's captain; and a few other courageous crew members left their shipmates on Elephant Island to undertake a journey in search of help. They sailed more than 800 miles over treacherous seas to South Georgia in a whaleboat. It took many weeks to find help and rescue the trapped crew on Elephant Island. Shackleton believed that they would live, return to England, and see their families again. The team endured many trials throughout their journey, including frostbite, starvation, and terrifying weather events, but not one member of the crew of the *Endurance* died. Shackleton exerted strong will in the face of unusual trials, and his amazing feat showed the power of extreme hope and perseverance in the face of seemingly insurmountable odds.

Mindset over Matter

Regardless of status or other characteristics, one can develop this kind of optimistic mindset. You can push past your perceived limits and persevere in the face of challenges and adversity. Your capacity to endure is much greater than you know. Perseverance is more a mental exercise than it is a physical one. While your body and your mind certainly have a breaking point, it is likely that you can do much more than you think you can at the point where you first experience resistance.

There is incredible power in your thoughts and mind. When you feel close to your breaking point, are running fast toward burnout, or just feel tired, you can take refuge in your mindset, which you can train to persevere. Revisit what you believe about yourself, and hopefulness and grit can help you overcome the challenge. Similar to, but distinct from, optimism, hope can be created and learned. Again, in his book *Making Hope Happen*, the late hope researcher Dr. Shane J. Lopez described hope as the belief that "the future will be better than the present" and that "I have the power to make it so." Lopez asserts that hope is malleable and transferrable to others, and there are tools available to help create a hopeful mindset, such as resetting your goals and doing more of what you do best.

While you may never experience a shipwreck in Antarctica nor become a POW, you will have days when you experience the proverbial "no way out" at some point in your life. The current reality may indeed include difficult circumstances and an uncertain future. This is the time to assess your mindset. Practice resolve. Practice believing that your purpose is reachable. Persevere through the hardship. Take the first next step toward fulfilling your purpose. Then take the next step. Continue to take reasonable next steps based on your current circumstances that move you closer to the positive future you are envisioning. Create a feedback loop in your mind where you revisit your thought-life and what you believe about yourself. Work hard at practicing optimism. Persevere each hour, each day, and each year. It will be worth the effort.

SECTION 3

Know Your Purpose

I hope at this point, you've examined your life, defined your priorities, and determined they will be lived—not just stated—priorities. I hope by now you can see the necessity of building good habits to be true to those priorities, starting with positive, clarifying thoughts and words and then taking action; building the effectiveness of those actions through practice; and being ready to demonstrate perseverance through challenges. These are perspectives and practices that are foundational to building your life on purpose. Now, prepare to bring your purpose into sharp focus.

CHAPTER 10

Eternally Minded

Your true purpose will be something you can do throughout your life, and something you can build a legacy around. To start, reflect on your past experiences and the moments when you were most focused. Dwell on the things you feel most passionate about. Consider the topics, activities, or context you encountered where your passion never waned. Then look to the future to see how and where you can direct that passion to make a difference throughout your life.

When I reflected on my earliest experiences, I realized I have always assumed leadership roles, even as a youngster. Among the four Nyffeler siblings, I typically directed construction of the family forts in the basement or planned the day's mischief. It was something that came naturally for me, but later I worked to grow and develop those skills in myself and others. Leading and helping others lead will continue to be central to my purpose throughout my life. In *Now, Discover Your Strengths*, Don Clifton, entrepreneur, researcher, and father of strengths-based psychology, studied how to help people identify their talent—those things they naturally do well that come most easily to them. To help discover your purpose, think about what you do best.

You may have a high degree of empathy, knowing what someone is feeling and experiencing, and understanding when to come alongside to offer support. You might have a proclivity for serving others and can spot when something needs to be done, even when others miss it. You are the one who steps in to fill the gap to get a project over the finish line, and you do so with a high level of commitment and joy. Or, you might always have the right words to steer and influence others. You create written words or speak in a way that brings clarity and understanding. You might be wise about when to use those words and when to remain quiet and listen. Or you may be skilled at making deep and lasting relationships. You help others feel valued and know ways to build meaningful connections that endure. You may be a deep thinker who can solve problems and identify the best solutions or spot the flaws in shaky ones.

Whatever they are, examine your experiences and consider when others have noticed your unique characteristics. Lean into the things that you can develop and leverage for the betterment of others, from birth to death.

Find What Sparks Joy

In addition to thinking about the things that you naturally do well, to clarify your purpose, reflect on those things in your life that bring you the most joy or a sense of fulfillment. Think about the actions you took and what marked the interactions you had in those moments. You may need to practice some solitude to reflect on the elements that best highlight your unique purpose. Introspection is easier for some people than others. If you have a trusted friend, family member, or partner, you might invite them to come alongside this process with you. If you are struggling to identify those things, take several weeks—or even a few months—and practice noticing. Notice things you tend to think about and do without anyone asking or inviting you to think about or do them. Notice the things others consistently approach you about or things that they need from you. Begin to sort the elements that bring you a sense of joy and fulfillment.

Think about what happens when you're in a group. Ask yourself which questions and topics you feel most confident answering or engaging with. When you volunteer, identify consistencies between the roles. Do you tend to organize, listen, communicate, make connections, expand networks, serve quietly, invite followers, or create new things? The more clarity you have on what you were uniquely created for, the more focused your purpose statement will be, the more intentionally you can craft your life in alignment with your purpose, and the more joy and fulfillment you will experience. You will be able to pursue the life for which you were uniquely designed and created—on purpose.

Knowing you have a purpose with an eternal focus should feel rewarding and exciting! You will feel excited and committed. When you describe your eternal purpose to friends or family members, it should energize you. At work, I enjoy offering different opportunities for colleagues to learn what really gets them engaged. While I care about outcomes of the projects or assignments, many people can perform well on tasks, even when they don't necessarily like them. So, instead, I'm watching what gets their full effort and attention. I'm looking for what gets them most energized and focused, a phenomenon that Hungarian American psychologist Mihaly R. Csikszentmihalyi describes in his book *Flow*. It is a lot of fun to watch people doing something they are made to do, where time passes without notice.

Your purpose should not only be eternal—something you can pursue for all of your days—it should also be a purpose with significance beyond yourself.

CHAPTER 11

Transcendent Aim

A s I've previously stated, your true purpose will have a relevance that transcends you. It will make a difference outside of yourself and will positively impact the world and the lives of others. The language of our culture is frequently infused with references to "me, myself, and I." There are countless songs and television personalities that exemplify such a focus. And while there is certainly merit to self-reflection and making oneself better, as I'm certainly advocating for in this book, the benefits of such growth shouldn't stop with you. Your growth as an individual frees you to pursue your eternal purpose, one that has reach beyond yourself.

Many products and services marketed in recent decades also focus on the self. This makes sense, since it's not likely we would spend money on things that don't help or improve our own lives. It has become normal to think this way. To sell razors, Gillette's tagline for many years, for example, was "Gillette. The best a man can get." L'Oréal Paris's tagline is

"Because you're worth it." Burger King's new tagline is reportedly "You rule," putting a fresh twist on their jingle "Have It Your Way."

A focus on oneself isn't new, really, but there does seem to me to be a cultural shift in values to elevate oneself over others. It was a tremendous time of self-sacrifice in the early-to-mid-twentieth century, when many engaged in service to their country to fight against tyranny in Europe and around the globe. A cultural icon at the time was Rosie the Riveter—first captured by artist J. Howard Miller in 1942. The image was titled "We Can Do It!" Rosie represented self-sacrifice and empowerment, and the campaign aimed to facilitate a movement of women out of their homes and into the workforce to support the war effort for the nation.

Over a period of twenty years of service to the country, George Washington did not spend much time at home. His life was marked by critical events that demanded inordinate amounts of time, courage, fortitude, and commitment. He courageously and strategically engaged in battle during the Revolutionary War, served as commander-in-chief of the Continental Army during the crafting of the Declaration of Independence, and skillfully navigated the political landscape to be unanimously elected the first president of the United States. Washington then served a second term but did not run for a third term, modeling a peaceful, intentional transfer of power for future administrations. George Washington's life work served a transcendent purpose, influencing generations of Americans and even those in other democratically oriented nation-states around the world.

A Legacy of Purpose

My heritage includes immigrant family members whose focus and purpose transcended their own lives. My great-great-grandfather immigrated to

Nebraska when he was only eighteen years old. I once returned to my family's ancestral homeland of Switzerland to learn more. My great-great-grandfather was from a family of farmers, but land was scarce. It was not possible for the family's acreage to be divided such that he and his three siblings could all live and thrive off it. Instead, he took the limited amount of cash his father had to spare and made the months-long journey to Nebraska.

When he arrived, he found work on the farm of a Swiss neighbor until he was eventually approved for some land of his own. Within months of arriving in America, he met his wife. They eventually married and started their own family. They labored diligently but lived in poverty, struggling to learn which crops would grow best, managing foreign and unpredictable weather patterns, and possessing no resources to construct a fully functional farm. He had four sons, and his whole existence was focused on creating a better life for them.

My great-great-grandfather could have remained solely focused on his own personal circumstances, but instead, he helped build a community that would not only improve the lives of his own family members but would also improve the lives of others. He started a church, as well as the first community school in that church. He did these things prior to constructing a permanent, proper house for himself and his family. Like others in that day and age, he attended to critical elements for his community ahead of his personal comfort. This is true in many historic areas and towns around the world. Some of the oldest, most well-constructed sites that remain standing are communal spaces, such as churches. Leaders who stepped up to create and construct those spaces had a transcendent focus. A significant part of their lives, as was the case for my ancestors, was oriented toward serving others' needs.

I continued researching my great-great-grandfather and the lives of his family members. I found early photographs of my great-grandfather and his farm, and I noticed three things in that photo. They had a large farm with a special garden. I was surprised to see vegetables sitting on the front porch beside the front door. I also noticed the rough state of their homestead. It looked destitute. It surprised me to see those vegetables sitting out exposed and vulnerable to the elements or animals.

I asked my grandparents about this. They explained, "Reed. The farm was your business. You spent every day trying to make a living, toiling on the farm. So, at the end of the season, you would have something to sell, and you could take that money to help build your life. That garden, you see, was your sustenance. It was the 'refrigerator' that you used daily to feed your family. Typically, the wife and mother tended to that garden, and you protected it with your life. If you didn't sell any products, your life would not be better, but if you lost that garden, you could lose your life."

But this didn't quite answer my question about why there was produce on the porch. They continued to explain that the vegetables on the porch were there as a gift to the community. Only people who desperately needed food to live would come and take those vegetables. My great-grandfather had very little, but even in poverty, it was a cultural expectation to support the community in some manner—to think transcendently beyond your own circumstances. My dad explained on several occasions that families actively supported and cared for those in need. By way of example, community members participated in barn raisings for families when the father became ill or injured. Mothers supported new mothers and came to help when their neighbors were nursing sick children back to health. It was common to see people living with open hearts and hands, advancing a mindset that their purpose in life transcended their own lived experience.

Living in Service to Others

My grandfather passed away about twenty years ago. I remember going to his house and hearing hard stories about their difficult lives on the farm. He would talk about each of the new items they acquired that helped to make daily life easier. As we were going to grandpa's funeral, my grandmother was clearly distraught. I happened to be the last to depart the house that day and wanted to help her. She loaded the car, and I went to lock up the house. I intended to drive my grandfather's truck into the garage, so of course I needed the keys. I didn't want to bother my grandmother about it, so I looked everywhere for those keys. As I searched in every drawer for those truck keys, they were nowhere to be found. Ultimately, I had no choice but to ask her where they might be. She answered, "Reed, we don't have a lock on our house. So, if anyone needs something, they can come in to get what they need from the refrigerator or garage. The keys are in the ignition of the truck, in case anyone ever needs to borrow it, they don't need to look for us or ask. They can just borrow it."

In my community today, we keep our keys inside our homes, in a safe place that is inaccessible to others. We also lock the doors to our home before we leave to ensure no one can gain access to our space. That moment with my grandmother was a powerful one that, to me, represents the epitome of a transcendent mindset—we exist, and our most important possessions exist—to serve and help others. My grandmother was still thinking about others' needs, even while grieving the loss of her husband of fifty years.

Your life purpose is to offer your gifts in service to others. It is possible, even in your most difficult moments of sorrow or grief, to consider others' needs. While the society around us may continue to elevate self-involvement and self-edification, you will not realize your most fulfilling and purposeful life if that is your only orientation. Well-being researchers have suggested that service to the community can be an important boost to personal well-being.[8] It is good for us to be good to others. To live a life on purpose, think of others ahead of yourself.

I truly believe that the last shall be first and the first shall be last, as Jesus noted. To become a person with a transcendent mindset, consider who you most instinctively think of first. Once you are eternally minded and have a transcendent aim, you can consider the next critical element of a strong statement of purpose and whether it can be universally applied in your life.

8   Susan Krauss Whitbourne, "How Caring About Others Benefits Your Own Mental Health," *Psychology Today*, August 24, 2021, https://www.psychologytoday.com/us/blog/fulfillment-any-age/202108/how-caring-about-others-benefits-your-own-mental-health.

CHAPTER 12

Universally Applied

The final pillar of your purpose statement is to make it universally applicable. Your purpose should be relevant to every context of your life. To experience fulfillment, you cannot compartmentalize your purpose. Your purpose is rooted in who you are created to be, your unique gifts, and your interests, so living your life on purpose should involve your whole self and your whole life.

I hope as you make your way along this journey, you have considered whether you are consistently yourself when practicing or expressing your faith, when you're with your family, when you're at work, volunteering, or having fun. As you've learned, my four priorities are faith, family, productivity, and rest and enjoyment. I imagine you may have similar priorities. Reflect on your priorities and each area of your life. If your priorities require you to be or act much differently in each place or space, you may not be living authentically in all of those areas. When I refer to living an authentic life, I simply mean being genuine and transparent in every space where you find yourself.

If your purpose is universally applicable, you will find the freedom to be authentically yourself regardless of the place or time. If you want to live out your faith, for example, but it is only a stated rather than a lived priority, you may feel uncomfortable and confused as you monitor your words and actions. You do not want to have a life that is only a show, as it will keep you from growing, and your confusion and discomfort will be recognizable to others.

Similarly, when you are with your family, if you feel you are walking on eggshells, or that you are being judged, take care and do the work to figure out what is driving those feelings and whether they are preventing you from living purposefully and authentically in that environment. While you cannot control others' perceptions, you can control your own thoughts, words, and actions. Ensure that they align with your purpose, and be willing to have (sometimes difficult) conversations with those closest to you to invite their perspectives. Share with them the ways you are adjusting your life and lifestyle to align with your purpose, so that they understand the purpose you aim to fulfill, and so you may live more authentically with them.

Continue finding ways to share your unique purpose at work. However, if you feel that you must guard your words and actions in that environment, or if you feel you cannot be genuine and authentic, you may be missing the chance to live most purposefully. If you lament going to work each day, or go only to collect a paycheck, you are likely not living your most purposeful life there. It could be that your perspective on your current job can shift, or you may find that where and how you work is something that can change over time. But together, all these spaces can provide insights and opportunity into what your universally applicable purpose could be.

View Your Hobbies Holistically

The ways you spend your free time relaxing and having fun can also shed light on what is most universal in your purpose. The amazing thing about free time is that there is less accountability, responsibility, or expectation around it. So you have great freedom to figure out what you clearly enjoy most and what might be good ways to apply your purpose.

I have a couple of hobbies I've nurtured for decades. First, I enjoy leading studies and facilitating conversations about the Bible. Since my teen years, I've gathered people who may be in a similar life stage to study different aspects of the Bible and engage in discussions that can help inform and enrich our lives. I participated in Christian organizations in high school and college, led a college Bible study, and hosted a group of young married couples, discussing God's heart and intent for marriage and families. In each of those life stages, I've enjoyed leading, fostering relationships, having conversations, and learning together.

I also enjoy playing basketball. In college, I spent the little free time I had at the gym. I'd find a group and play competitive pickup games. Even after college, I looked for a gym and still occasionally play with a group of guys on Saturday mornings. In each of those settings, regardless of my athleticism, which admittedly has been blunted as the years go by, I enjoy helping to make my team better. I might work on setting screens to enable someone else to score or focus on securing rebounds so I can get the ball out to the open person. Sometimes I just joke around to lighten the mood or encourage a new player as they work to fit into the scheme.

Of course, I also want to live out my purpose at Signal. My work as the CEO has included learning ways to best lead people, and helping people learn to lead—at scale—was a key part of my vision for the company. While the business is global, I also live out this same intent and purpose at home with my family. My children can attest to the fact that in many (perhaps most) of our conversations, I encourage them to find ways to learn, grow, and become each day—to identify their skills, interests, and capacity and to act, practice, and persevere as they pursue their own purpose.

During a particularly big career transition in my mid- to late thirties, I realized my intent to lead and develop leaders could be universally integrated into every area of my life. I could always be my authentic self as I leveraged my thoughts and actions toward that purpose. I hope that you, too, will develop an eternal and transcendent mindset as you craft your purpose, and that it will be one that is universally applicable in all areas of your life, so that you can always be authentically you in all places. Once you are ready to adopt that eternal and universal mindset and commit to a purpose that can be universally applied in all areas of your life, you can begin crafting your unique statement of purpose that will guide your life.

CHAPTER 13

Make a Statement

My purpose statement provides that proverbial north star, enabling me to sort where my time and energy can best be focused. It offers clarity and direction and freedom, also, to *not* pursue everything because time and energy are finite. I hope that you, too, will land on a succinct and clear purpose statement that *frees* you to authentically do and be what you were uniquely created for, and that you will be continually energized as you fulfill that purpose.

Again, my purpose statement is "through intuitive interaction, propel leaders through their self-imposed barriers to live out their unique purpose in life." My purpose will be consistent throughout my life. It is transcendent in that it is innately focused on helping other leaders. My purpose can be pursued and applied universally within the context of each of my priorities: faith, family, work, and even rest and recreation.

The Four Elements of a Purpose Statement

Your purpose statement should reflect an eternal and transcendent mindset and include elements that can be universally applied in all areas of your life. Your life priorities and the habits you are developing to honor those priorities on a consistent basis should inform your purpose statement. It will encourage you to think quite concretely about who you are, how you intend to live your life, and how you wish to be remembered. You will carefully craft each word of your purpose statement that will serve as your compass to help you intentionally live your life on purpose.

1. How Will You Apply Your Purpose?

To begin your statement, think about *how* you will apply your purpose. For me, I wanted to leverage interactions with others, so I began my own statement with the phrase "Through intuitive interaction . . ." Intuitive interaction, for me, stems from spending years practicing sorting information for the most salient data points. It includes listening intently and paying particular attention to nonverbal communication and cues and understanding context or other information to figure out what is most important and what the underlying message is. For example, I enjoy observing others' talent and passion at work, and figuring out when they are truly engaged and excited about what they are doing. I use those skills and context clues to help inform ways to encourage and propel leaders forward. It helps me determine whether I will be applying my time in a way that aligns with my purpose.

As you craft your purpose statement, think about ways for you to recognize whether an opportunity merits your time and energy because it aligns with your purpose and then put words to that filter. Perhaps you will do this "through researching," or "by exploring new places," or "by thinking through scenarios and possibilities," or "by gauging sentiment and perceptions," or "through empathetic listening." Your way of sorting a possibility and whether it aligns with your purpose will be rooted in your own skills and abilities. This first element of your purpose statement gives you a starting point for applying your purpose in each context.

2. What Do You Want to Do?

The second element of your purpose statement should clearly state what you want to do. My life purpose is to "propel leaders." I have always been drawn to leadership and leaders. It is a succinct aim to move leaders forward and keep them from getting bogged down by barriers that might arise. I know that when I support them in their personal and professional growth, that leadership is multiplied, which can positively influence many other lives.

What you want to do, again, should be rooted in what you do best and what brings you joy and fulfillment. Perhaps you want to help hurting or struggling people, console the brokenhearted, steer others' financial decisions, improve systems—the possibilities for your purpose are unlimited. Your words should reflect what you are passionate about, and when you are doing it, time stands still. You've selected the right sentence when you realize it describes something that you can envision yourself doing all the days of your life. Choose the words that truly energize you.

3. What Approach Will You Take?

The next element that your purpose statement should include is the approach you will consistently take to fulfill what you want to do. Again, my purpose is to "propel leaders," and I have considered the way that I can best do that. I sensed in my work and personal experiences that one of the primary challenges leaders face is figuring out how to identify and overcome self-imposed barriers. Therefore, this is my primary focus and method. As I listen to leaders eager to grow and maximize their own purpose and potential, I'm intently listening for clues to what might be holding them back—barriers that they have constructed for themselves that might be limiting them. I aim to help them discover what they can change about their mindsets that could help them achieve the results and outcomes they want. This part of my purpose statement provides further clarity about how I fulfill my purpose with leaders.

Your approach, again, will be different from mine. It could include sharing encouragement, donating time or resources, walking alongside, developing plans, or helping others start or break habits. It is impossible to name all the possible methods you could state and employ for your purpose statement. Just ensure that the words reflect a tangible approach you can consistently take. The more succinct and clear this element of your purpose statement is, the better and more frequently you can apply it. As you pursue living your life on purpose, you will become more adept, and your influence and impact will increase!

4. When Is Your Purpose Fulfilled?

The fourth and final element of your purpose statement is a phrase that helps you know when you have fulfilled your role and purpose within a given context. It bears reminding that you cannot be all things to everyone. In fact, if you attempt to do that, you will likely be robbing someone else of the chance to contribute their own purpose. In my purpose statement, the final phrase is "to live out their unique purpose in life." This, again, is clarifying for me. When I see someone who has a new or renewed sense of their purpose, the barriers they have constructed are removed, and they are actively pursuing it. Then I know I've accomplished my role.

I liken the experience to a bird being nudged out of the nest once its wings are strong enough for it to take that first leap. Once a leader has that first experience of freedom from their barrier and has a vision of the possibilities, then it is time for me to support the next person. Think about how you know that you've accomplished your purpose first, so you can really appreciate and take some joy in fulfilling that purpose, and so you can be on the lookout for others who could step into a next phase and share their purpose.

For many, it can be difficult to know when to reallocate your energy and time to fulfill your purpose somewhere else. But this element of your purpose statement is critical. There will be relationships in your life that are forever. However, even those you love most will require others in their world to enable them to succeed and be successful. It is healthy to know and understand that you have particular gifts and that you have a particular purpose for using them. Your energy and time are not infinite. God alone has infinite power and capacity. So, while the ending to your purpose statement will be different from mine, I encourage you to name the time or indicator that will enable you to share the next phase with someone else. Your purpose is eternal (can serve for a lifetime and leave a legacy), it is transcendent (has influence beyond yourself), and it is universal (applicable in each area of your life). Figure out how to determine when it is time to put your purpose to good use in a new context or with new people.

I am hopeful that I will leave a positive legacy built on my purpose statement. I hope that in each of the priorities of my life—my faith, my family, my work, and even my free time—whomever I've interacted with would say, "Reed helped me to have a better life. He listened to me and propelled me forward so that I could live a more purposeful life."

Similarly, I hope that as you craft your own statement to steer your life on purpose, you will have more focus and clarity—that your purpose statement would truly be motivating, exciting, and life-giving. I hope it feels worth pouring your whole self and your whole life into!

Once you have that statement—or a very good start—you are ready to start managing your time to live out that life on purpose.

Start Your Journey on Purpose

Now that you have your priorities identified, an approach for developing habits to faithfully honor your priorities, and an eternal, transcendent, universally applicable purpose statement to guide you, you're ready to begin the intentional journey of living your life on purpose. You will learn to put thoughtful structure around your life to maximize the opportunity to fulfill your life on purpose. And you will start by keeping the end in mind.

CHAPTER 14

Long-Term Vision

Maintain a long view for your living your life on purpose. This journey is not a sprint. My daughter E2, like E1, is also a very good runner. She mostly ran distance to keep in shape for soccer. She began her cross-country races with the back half of the 5K in mind and paced herself accordingly. Similarly, you should approach the fulfillment of your purpose with a long-term vision. Think carefully about the implications of having such a focused direction for your life. Imagine, if you currently have children, for example, what your children will tell their children and even their grandchildren about you? What might your former colleagues tell their coworkers? What is it that you would like them to be able to say? What core and lasting memories do you hope they have of you? These kinds of concrete questions about your legacy can help inform the ways that you apply your energy each day.

As a teen, I was one of just a few of my friends to have a living grandparent. Remarkably, my great-grandma Adeline and great-grandpa Henry on my mother's side were also both living at the time and well into their nineties. I had so much respect for them, and I'm grateful I had the chance to know them. They celebrated seventy-five years of marriage, and were as loving, committed, and adorable an elderly couple as you could imagine. They possessed such a wealth of knowledge, history, and life experience. The wisdom emanated from them. As I reflect now, roughly thirty years after their deaths, their legacy of steadfast commitment and love still shapes me.

Modeling a Legacy

My great-grandparents were not wealthy, so they didn't leave a legacy of material things. It was not their stature in the community or fame that left its mark, though Great-grandfather did own a small convenience store for many decades in a small Nebraska town, so many people far and wide knew him. It was not necessarily the delicious cooking and meals that Great-grandmother prepared, though her grands and great-grands always enjoyed every single bite of her wholesome homemade dishes. The imprint they left on our minds and memories—the defining element of their legacy—was truly their hearts. Their hearts were bent toward service, encouragement, and love. They modeled that for all their family and friends, and it will be remembered always.

I'd been to my great-grandparents' home many times for just about every holiday that I could remember, enjoying Thanksgiving meals and Christmases. We all looked forward to receiving slippers each year. Great-grandmother knitted slippers for every family member every year—at least thirty pairs of slippers! She wanted to share a gift that showed her care, but she didn't have money to purchase unique gifts for everyone. This was one of my most treasured gifts at Christmas each year. She always asked what color we preferred, and even with arthritis in her fingers, she would knit all of those slippers. It must have taken her the entire year.

When I was about eight or nine years old, my parents went on a vacation and left my four-year-old sister, my two brothers (seven and eight years), and I with my great-grandparents. We were there for about one week. It was such an impactful week in my life. That week gave me insight into true servant-hearted leadership—their lasting legacy. I witnessed and experienced firsthand their kindness and gentleness that they treated one another with. They expended their energy to care for the fourth generation of high-energy Nyffeler boys and my young sister. They invested many special moments with each of us, realizing that they were sowing precious, lasting seeds of moments and memories, as their lives were nearing the end.

One of the last meals that we shared with my great-grandparents before my parents returned from their trip serves as a memory that I'll never forget. We kids had requested some of my great-grandmother's special bread. It was a difficult task and a lot of work for her. She toiled many hours during the holidays to make it. But without hesitation, she said yes. However, she was missing some of the ingredients that she needed to bake it. My great-grandfather was nearly deaf at this point in his life from years of laboring and having minimal regard for his own health. So my great-grandfather did not have a driver's license. He got around town on his three-wheeled bicycle. Since my great-grandmother had a lot of work to do, my great-grandfather decided to bike to the grocery store in town, bringing all four of us with him. My sister sat in the basket up front. My seven-year-old brother stood on the cross bar in back, as he held on to Great-grandfather's shoulders. My brothers and I switched off hopping on and off the back of that bike with the other two running and walking alongside him. My great-grandfather, regardless of how old or tired he may have felt, pedaled as fast as we could run, even carrying all of that weight on that bike. No matter the trials and tribulations he encountered, Great-grandfather would never complain. He simply got to work caring for everyone. We finally returned with the needed ingredients, and he delivered them with a smile. That is the legacy that I'll remember always.

This picture of my great-grandparents, that forever lives in my memories, causes me to think long term about what I hope to invest in future generations. I want my long-term vision to steer the way I spend my energy until my dying days. I want to be just like my great-grandfather—servant-hearted in a way that others may not even be aware of the sacrifices made for their sake. I want to love my wife as he loved his, willing to drop everything at any time without complaint to serve her and his family, investing each ounce of energy at every opportunity. That is my long-term vision for living my life on purpose.

Choosing a Vision for the Future

Consider a picture of someone's life that you hope to emulate, someone whose legacy you admire. I challenge you to create a long-term vision— a picture that helps inform the plans for your days and your years. It might be personified by a family member, or perhaps a member of the community whom you've been observing and admire. Or perhaps, you've not had the opportunity to see a worthwhile legacy modeled, and you need to construct one yourself. Whichever avenue you take to create your own vision of the far future, make sure it is a clear picture—one that is aspirational for you. It ought to make you smile to see it in your mind's eye.

When I attended my great-grandfather's funeral, a few years after that bike ride to the grocery store, the whole community turned out to share their condolences and show their respect. My whole family was present, and as a new believer in Christ at that time, I could hear God say about my great-grandfather, "Well done, my good and faithful servant. Yours was a life well-lived." As we were deciding what to pass along to the family members, when we were sorting through my great-grandparents' possessions, I requested to have his Bible. I knew that his life was based upon the principles and priorities that he had established as a young man of faith, who cared for his family, worked well and hard, and enjoyed life. I recognized that could be my template on which I could model my own long-term vision. I do hope you have a literal picture—a long-term vision—that motivates you to wake up running toward it each day.

CHAPTER 15

Five-Year Milestone

Now that you have a picture of your long-term vision, it is time to create a plan to allocate your energy and where you will spend it over the first five years. You will want to set a five-year milestone. Five years may feel like a long time, so setting up some regular checkpoints to assess your progress will be critical. Research shows that setting milestones—goals with descriptors—is an exercise in practicing hopefulness. My oldest daughter, E1, was quite an accomplished runner in junior high and high school. She was always fast, even as a young girl. She began beating me at foot races when she was in seventh grade—a first peek at my own mortality. As she got older, other kids started getting faster and catching up with her. So she moved from running the 100-meter dash to the 400-meter dash. That race, while still considered a "dash," which I frankly think is a misnomer, is not exactly an all-out sprint, like the 100-meter is. It required her to adjust her speed and pacing to ensure she could maintain speed across a much greater distance.

The great thing about track is that the distance, whether it's a sprint or a distance race, is always the same for everyone. Everyone has the same distance for which they need to apportion their energy. Runners who can train at a high level and learn to pace themselves will achieve their goals and the outcomes they want. In a similar way, everyone has a finite amount of energy, and you need to know when to apply it in quick bursts to pace yourself to achieve your best performance. The longer the distance, the more critical it is to learn how to pace and manage your energy and remain focused on the finish line.

I was never a runner, so I had a lot to learn about the sport when my kids began running. High school cross country (XC) is a 5,000-meter race across various types of terrain. After watching E1 run track, and E2 run XC, it was clear that the goal for all races was to cross that finish line as quickly as possible. However, the way you approach those races in terms of preparation and racing strategy is completely different. For longer distances, it is imperative to measure and track your pace and learn to expend and adjust your energy as needed. In sprint races on the track, you can see where you stand relative to other athletes in the race. However, for long distance races, such as a cross country 5K or a half or full marathon, you need to be very tuned in to what your body needs and what your effort should be to stay on pace because sometimes you are on your own. It is possible you won't see the next closest runner to you in the race, since the course is spread out across such a large distance. That is why setting your goals and knowing your splits is critical to be sure you are on pace for the time you want to hit.

Take Aim at Your Milestone

The first big milestone in your purpose journey will be five years out. With a long-term vision and a purpose statement to guide you, you should document what success looks like for you five years from now. It is important to set a target. My dad taught me to shoot targets with my BB gun when I was young. Once I learned to line up the notch near to my eye with the notch at the end of the barrel, I could be reasonably sure that my aim was pretty close to where the shot would end up on the target. The principle holds true for your five-year milestone for your purpose. Figure out what you are aiming for, see it in your sights, and write it down.

As you set your five-year milestone, make sure it is reachable and challenging. A simple example is perhaps your purpose is to help others make connections. Describe what success looks like in five years for this purpose—describe how many and what types of connections you hope to have facilitated. If you are a mile runner, and you want to be under a five-minute mile, you will need to complete each lap in one minute and fifteen seconds. If you fall behind that first lap right out of the gate, you will have to pick up that pace and actually run faster than your intended pace to catch up. At some point, catching up to your intended pace will not be possible if you don't hit it early.

By now, it won't surprise you to know that I love watching the Olympics and that, like many, swimming always has my attention. It is incredibly competitive, and swimmers spend years and thousands of hours swimming laps and doing other training regimens to prepare. It is particularly exciting to watch races that have the digitally generated line that tracks along with the lead swimmer in the race. That line shows the required pace for an Olympic or world record pace. While the swimmer, of course, can't see that line, the television spectators see this "invisible" race with the imaginary swimmer who already made history. It helps us know in real time that history is once again being made. Your five-year milestone should be like that—an exciting challenge that keeps you engaged and making progress that you can assess.

Set your milestone so that it can be your own personal world record for your life. Don't set a milestone that is easily achievable, but do set one that you can absolutely envision achieving. Again, make that long-term view a picture that you can see in your mind. Billie Jean King has been credited with saying, "If you can see it, you can be it," as she advocated for fair and equal treatment for women in professional tennis. The rationale is that visualizing something for yourself, or seeing it realized in someone's life with whom you can closely identify, provides the mindset and motivation required to succeed.

I remember setting such a milestone for the first time around my late teen years, and I was pretty specific about my goals. I had a significant financial earnings goal; I wanted to own a home of my own; I hoped to be married and to have children by the time I was in my early thirties. Those goals lived inside my own mind. I never shared them with anyone—before now—because they were very personal. The goals aligned with my priorities of having a family, and it was important to me to provide well for their needs. Once I set the goals, I looked at my current situation and made a plan. I knew I needed to go to college, and that if I wanted to be married one day, I needed to begin dating. As a junior in high school, I had my plan to graduate from college and find a job at a large company and jumpstart my career being a productive contributor.

Once I had made those decisions and set my goals, it helped the decision-making feel easier in the interim. All decisions for my life would run through the filter of my milestone goals to see if or how it could help get me closer to the goal, or if it would lead me further away. When people feel lost and unsure, it is often because they don't have a good look at what their long-term milestone vision is, so they don't know what to do in the short term. I set a few interim milestones along the way to my goals. I shared a few of them, which I was able to achieve, namely, graduating from college, and I did begin to date someone, and later was engaged to be married. I also secured and gained experience in a role at a growing company.

Write It Down!

To ensure your success, you need to record your five-year milestone. Make sure you first have your purpose statement recorded in a place where you can easily see and read it. Then either record or write your long-term vision as discussed in the previous chapter. If you're an artist, you might paint a picture of what the best possible future could be. Write drafts on notecards, use a whiteboard, or create a document on your device. Your five-year milestone should not be theoretical. Make it concrete and tangible. Make it clear (i.e., easy to understand and makes sense), memorable (i.e., succinct so you can repeat it and not need a cheat sheet), measurable (i.e., you can use numbers, graphics, or descriptors that are indicators of success), and portable (i.e., it doesn't live on a proverbial shelf but can be relevant in each of your circumstances). And it should absolutely include the kinds of experiences and stories you want to be able to share with others.

Building on an example that I shared earlier, suppose your purpose statement is: "Through volunteerism and professional engagements, build relational networks that support strong educational outcomes for students that set them on a path to success." If this is your purpose statement, your five-year milestone might look like: "Join or engage with up to three nonprofit boards and a professional network that support education-related causes and/or educators and make up to twenty-five new connections across those organizations and relationships." You might need to determine or decide what qualifies as a "connection" and why that matters, but the example is concrete, and it includes potential spaces. If your priorities include an element of work, this goal may align well. If you have priorities that conflict with spending the requisite time to join and serve on boards, then your milestone may need to look different. Find avenues for your goals that already intersect with the priorities you've established.

Finally, many things in life happen outside of our control. If that happens, reassess and recreate your milestone. But a greater risk than setbacks is missing the opportunity to fulfill your purpose in a big way because you did not have a vision for what could be and a plan to get there. So be sure your milestone will push you and challenge you. Be sure it will require your best energy and lead you to start fulfilling the purpose you stated over time. Once you have set a five-year milestone, you're ready to think about your annual checkpoint!

CHAPTER 16

Annual Checkpoint

Once your five-year milestone is defined, you will work backward from there and determine what your progress checkpoint should look like after year one. The intent is to keep yourself accountable for positive movement toward your purpose.

For decades, on or around my birthday on January tenth, I have taken time to review my progress toward living my life on purpose—a personal purpose inventory. Within the last ten years, I formalized this a little more and included, as part of the process, a vision trip. It is designed to take me out of my typical places for personal and work life, to a place that has history, geography, business, or other elements that pique my interest or have potential to inspire new or different thinking around my purpose and priorities. By way of example, I recently took a vision trip to West Virginia. It was the only US state I had yet to visit at the time. On that trip, I went to Harpers Ferry, where John Brown, a passionate abolitionist, made his raid on the federal armory with the intent of beginning a revolt to end slavery. Later, in 1862, President Abraham Lincoln stayed at Harpers Ferry to visit troops nearby, following one of the bloodiest battles of the Civil War several weeks earlier at Sharpsburg, Maryland. His visit helped him make critical personnel and strategic decisions that would not have been as informed had he remained in Washington. These events were reminders to me of the necessity to be present, to see, and to act.

It helps to layer the vision trip with my personal purpose inventory, to help me ideate potential ways that I can accelerate progress on my goals or even initiate new goals that are more aligned with my five-year milestone. Inevitably, I have valuable learnings around leadership, people, history, or other unexpected things that inform my purpose. I now enjoy taking vision trips to a new destination internationally. I come away with fresh perspectives simply by seeing, hearing, and otherwise experiencing things I never have before.

Successfully Passing the Checkpoint

The annual checkpoint requires preparation. Think ahead about exactly when you will do your personal purpose inventory, and what you will be asking yourself to assess your progress. Prepare to note each area of movement and progress. The checkpoint should leave you feeling energized and even more focused. Again, the vision trips that I've taken help to infuse that new energy and excitement for me, but perhaps you will best accomplish this same end through a quiet, intentional retreat or visit to a local favorite spot.

If you've ever been through a literal checkpoint, you know they can be a bit stress-inducing. If you've ever traveled in an airport, gone through customs in another country, crossed a border in a vehicle, or visited a military base or other secure facility, you've likely passed through a checkpoint. Scrutiny is part of the experience at checkpoints. For your annual purpose checkpoint, *you* are bringing scrutiny to the process and being honest about your progress. A little stress around that process is good. It means that it matters, and that you do have the ability to shift if needed.

Too much stress at a checkpoint, however, isn't fun. And being unprepared for that experience will escalate your stress. When traveling to other countries—some large, some small—of course, they have checkpoints and border officials patrolling them. Sometimes I take for granted that I can travel so widely within the continental US with relative ease for vacation and work. Of course, it is more restrictive and not as easy to pass through such checkpoints in many countries. On one trip early in my career, I was a little too confident and maybe naïve about my travel abilities, so I did not take into consideration the requirements for the country that I was traveling to. It was a serious glitch in my travel plans.

I quickly learned that each country requires a specific visa and I had to report exactly where I was planning to visit. In some places, you must disclose where you plan to stay and indicate a documented departure date with airline name and flight number. It was necessary to plan every detail well in advance of traveling to the country to ensure that each piece of information could be readily communicated, or you would be unable to enter and conduct business. After that early travel snag in my career, I became very intentional about the preparation needed to get through those checkpoints successfully, researching laws and regulations and preparing accordingly so I don't get stuck.

For my annual vision trip, I plan every detail, and ensure I account for where I'm staying, who is traveling with me, and the locations to visit. On that trip, I review my five-year milestone and the plan I've made to get there. I adjust it by adding another year to the five-year milestone. I review what has been accomplished in the last year and what things are left undone. I note things that have moved along according to the plan, and things that have not progressed as intended. I evaluate the checkpoint and why I determined the original goal or goals to begin with, and I make note of things that I learned along the way. Every year has something important and unique that helps me learn. I embrace that, even for years where the hoped-for outcomes didn't materialize. Every year of the journey is different and that is really the beauty of it.

Assessing and Adapting

It is important as you review the year, that you are prepared to adjust. Sometimes people spend too much energy resisting change—energy you could be leveraging toward the changes needed. Your purpose statement will remain consistent, but throughout each season of pursuing your purpose, you'll make changes in the pathways or methods you take to realize it. Be ready to make appropriate changes that steer you toward accomplishing your long-term vision and fulfilling your purpose.

During my annual checkpoint I also consider who I've interacted with over the previous year. I consider the impact on people's lives, note those that have come alongside me on the journey, as well as those who have exited my circle of influence. I think about where there may be gaps to fill with new talent and skills. My purpose statement is all about people. The review of people is the most critical step for me in my annual checkpoint. This involves the greatest amount of my time and thinking so I can figure out how to propel more leaders. While some relationships will last a lifetime, others may change and people may move, but there are always fresh opportunities to develop new, meaningful relationships. My review of my purpose and the previous year results in more clarity and direction and again, a renewed energy to pursue it.

So, I encourage you to plan an annual checkpoint to review progress on your life purpose and five-year milestone. Choose the right time of year and a place where you can take that personal purpose inventory. Again, your personal purpose inventory is a chance to ask yourself hard questions about the previous year, note where you have seen progress on your goals, and reflect on who has been a part of your journey. It will help you know where you are in the process of realizing your long-term vision for your life. Think about the decisions you have made and ask yourself if they have helped move you closer to your five-year milestone. Be sure to move out that milestone one year, adjusting the elements of the goals to be sure you're moving forward in living your life on purpose.

NOTE: The Appendix includes a tool with a short series of questions you can select from to aid your reflections.

CHAPTER 17

Quarterly Calibration

It isn't enough to have annual checkpoints on the way to your five-year milestone. You need to conduct quarterly calibrations to ensure progress on your purpose. In business, I've always enjoyed quarterly reviews most. It feels like just the right amount of time to have a tangible sense of how the business is doing. From day to day, it feels difficult to quantify progression or regression. And at the one-year mark, it is sometimes difficult to recall things that happened at the beginning of the year to know how it has changed. However, focusing on the previous few months seems like an appropriate amount of time to reflect upon what has happened, what you've done, and what decisions you've made, while also being able to project forward and generate excitement about the next few months.

If you only review the progress you are making on your purpose on an annual basis, it may be difficult to remain attentive to needed changes or opportunities. Over the course of a year, some details may be foggy and difficult to recall. However, if you build in quarterly calibrations to review the previous quarter and make adjustments for the upcoming quarter, your stated purpose will remain more vivid and relevant in your life. It will become a meaningful cadence that is reinforced by the habit of reflecting, planning, and changing course, as needed. As an aside, we humans seem to like divisions that include four parts to a whole: four quarters in a dollar, four quarters in a football game, four seasons in a calendar year, and four quarters in a fiscal year. Quarterly calibration of your goals and the plan to fulfill your purpose is a strong approach to ensuring ongoing progress.

I have found that in pursuing my purpose, if I consider each quarter the same way, I won't necessarily make the progress that I want to by the time my annual checkpoint rolls around. Sports competitions are a good illustration of this. For example, professional and collegiate men's basketball games are broken up into four quarters with a pause between quarters. The first quarter is when teams find out what works with their offense or what needs adjusting with the defense. They are trying to set a pace for the game. At the end of the second quarter, the teams want to make sure they keep the game close going into halftime so they are set up with a good chance to win. At halftime, coaches adjust so the team is better positioned to earn a win. In the third quarter, they are implementing adjustments and trying to create new momentum so that they are building energy moving into the fourth and final quarter. In the fourth quarter, there is strong attention to managing the team's energy, as fatigue can begin to play a big factor in executing the game plan, and depending on foul trouble or other factors, coaches are working to maximize the talents of the right players at exactly the right moments. There is also strong attention to managing the clock to ensure that every possession is a good possession and has the result of the final score needed to win the game.

How to Know, Sow, Grow, and Show

There are four steps I use for each quarter's calibration that help with the reflection on each of the checkpoints: Know, Sow, Grow, and Show. These align with each ninety-day period, starting January first, as the first quarter kicks off for me, each year, around my birthday and scheduled vision trip.

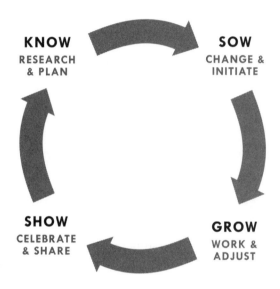

1. Know

This step involves creating a specific plan for the year of what I want to accomplish and is aligned with the long-term vision. Each year, I take three to five purpose-driven checkpoint items that I want to accomplish for that year. Then in quarter one, I thoroughly research them to understand the materials, resources, people, or other needs that are required to make it happen. I think about who can help me accomplish those aims and the time it will take to make it happen. At the end of the quarter, there is complete clarity on a plan, what is needed to operationalize it, and a schedule to know when it will be completed. It is clear what I need to know and what I need to do next.

2. Sow

The second step involves sowing the seeds of growth and progress by working the plan. Sometimes this quarter is the most frustrating. It may involve change and starting something new, so those around us may be confused and unsure of what to expect. If the plan involves changing a habit, schedule, or behavior, or includes adding in a new event or engagement that has never been a part of your life before, your energy, mind, body, and circle of influence will sense the shifts and changes. Even if positive, change often evokes trepidation or even fear. It can also feel like a challenging season because kicking off a plan is not synonymous with experiencing growth—at least not yet. You might not see growth or progress right away, so it might feel a little underwhelming. But remember, laying a foundation that sometimes people won't see is a critical and necessary first step to seeing a return and making progress. If you do not take time to plant the seeds of your growth by doing the little things that big growth requires, your purpose will elude you, remaining ethereal instead of lived.

3. Grow

The third step includes nurturing the seeds of the plan we have sown. As ideas take root and actions spur on other possibilities in your life, you adjust time and energy accordingly. Continue calibrating—revisiting your plan and taking the right steps to make it happen. If one idea or initiative you've started takes more time and energy, consider where you might save time and energy somewhere else. The same way farmers fertilize their fields and irrigate them to encourage those seeds to sprout, remove weeds that will choke out their fruit-bearing plants, and detassel their crops to maximize production yields, you need to nurture your ideas. Pay close attention to what they are yielding and whether it is what you expected or hoped. What adjustments might you make to help an idea come to life? If you take a break at this point in the journey and cease to pay attention to how things are playing out, you may stunt the process. Persist, so that you can see the harvest and fullest returns on the ideas that you set to work planning at the beginning of the year.

4. Show

Everyone wishes that they had something to show on day one. It would be great if we could simply think an idea and a plan into action and reap results immediately. But alas, we know it doesn't work that way. So do not reap the harvest before it's ready. Spend the time investing in and nurturing your ideas and initiatives. Give them time to take root and be fully developed. The Show is the most rewarding phase to be sure, but you cannot enjoy it without first initiating a strong plan, helping it take root, and nurturing it fully so that you can enjoy a harvest from your labor. I do encourage you to figure out what the Show means for you. It could be a big or meaningful but small "reveal" of your accomplishments. Depending upon what your goals were for your first annual checkpoint, it could be something others will readily notice, or it could be a privately achieved win. Figure out a way to celebrate and document it.

As you consider the following year—year two of your five-year milestone—break each year down into these four areas: Know, Sow, Grow, and Show. Ask yourself what you need to know to accomplish the goals—what research and knowledge is required? Create a detailed plan for initiating the work. Consider the right moment to start operationalizing your plan—to begin to sow those seeds of progress in quarter two. Then, be ready to initiate a third quarter calibration that involves nurturing and shifting the plan, so you have a clear path to the result you want to show at the end of the year.

CHAPTER 18

Monthly Measurement

The word "month" is derived from an Old English word, which means "moon," and early astronomers noted it took about twenty-nine or so days for the moon to rotate around the earth. We're all beneficiaries of calendars that today help us stay on track for where we are each year. So, the next way to ensure you are tracking toward your quarterly goals is to keep monthly measurements of your progress on your quarterly and annual goals. I want you to master each month so you can prioritize what matters.

Ever since we got married, my wife, Dana, has kept a detailed family calendar. When she flips each month, she records critical events and holidays for that whole month. She includes faith-based activities and events, such as weekly Bible study and youth group meetings. She includes immediate and extended family events and engagements. She studies the kids' school calendars to add engagements such as parent-teacher conferences, half days or full days off, and finally, adds the kids' extracurricular events for sports and clubs. I realize we're not unique in maintaining a regular and strict calendaring cadence each month for our family, but it's worth explicitly stating that this level of planning and coordination, especially when all six Nyffelers were still living under one roof, was critical to helping maximize our time, ensure we followed through with commitments, and reserved the support and energy we needed for one another and those outside of our immediate family.

While Dana isn't necessarily as passionate as I am about stating and documenting her personal purpose statement, she is very intentional on a monthly, weekly, and daily basis to live it out—starting with the way she writes each of the elements into the calendar according to her top priorities. I've always appreciated that she will document significant happenings on the calendar, even if they weren't necessarily planned ahead of time. She will record impromptu doctor appointments due to injury or illness, or the arrival time of a repair person if an appliance needs to be fixed at the house. The documentation serves to remind and inform, potentially, for follow-up or future needs, or for reference at some point in the future. Our family calendar, measuring and recording time and happenings, month by month, serves as a valuable tool to maintain a focus on our priorities and to ensure our time and energies are earmarked toward our collective purpose.

Mapping Your Near Future

Similarly, you will need to create a map of your life over the next quarter to ensure you are ready for those quarterly calibrations. You should take your quarterly plan and identify events, practices, time, and other measures of success for each of those three months. Begin with your top priority, which, for me, is my faith. I know, throughout each month, when I will be going to my local church or hosting a small group or investing personal time in growing my faith. Then I add family events and engagements, such as lunchtime with my wife. I include events that I'll actually attend, but I also include some that only others in my family will be attending but are important for me to be sure to talk with them about. I then add time that I have planned—or am simply available—for work travel, and of course, include those regular in-office days with requisite meetings. I add holidays and other planned days off, and finally, include times for recreation and other rest times for those open slots during some evenings and weekends.

Perhaps to you, this feels tedious, or perhaps you do this to some extent but not so intentionally. I encourage you to try it, as I think it will do a couple of things for you. It will ensure you begin to truly value all the days and weeks that you have. Because they are indeed limited. And it will help you know that you can include the most important things in your schedule to ensure you make progress on your purpose. This is what it means to schedule your priorities into your vision.

My wife adheres diligently to the calendar and has well-developed habits to review and update it as needed. She reviews the activities and knows when we've accomplished the week's aims and that we're making progress toward the next quarter of our lives. She studies it ahead of time—sometimes the night before or after the kids head off to school—it gives her clarity on what she wants to accomplish and helps her know she is making progress toward her vision to support our family in fulfilling each of our respective priorities.

It is imperative for you to do similarly if you are serious about an intent to live your life on purpose. The power of a monthly calendar that documents your intent regarding events and indicators of success is that you can visualize and plan the specific things that you need to do over the month to help you build those habits that set you on the path toward accomplishing your purpose (e.g., call four health clubs to get quotes for membership, invite three friends in my desired industry to coffee and write down three questions to help me learn). So, schedule those things you need to do. Whatever it is, put it in your monthly calendar!

You may need to shift your approach in the *way* you allocate your time and schedule it. Don't let things *happen* to you and your schedule. Be proactive. And think about the ways you reference and use your calendar and, therefore, your time. Don't default to letting things outside of you dictate your schedule. Make sure your priorities are rightly represented throughout the month. It's similar to the drive-through window at a fast-food restaurant. If you communicate ahead of time, very clearly, what you want when you order, it's—at least—more likely you will receive what you want. If you forget or otherwise neglect to order in the detail you need, you can't expect to get what you want.

Your calendar is like that menu of possible items to order. Be sure to organize your time and order your life around what you most want to get out of it. Then there is a much higher likelihood that, as each week's events arrive, you will experience the fulfillment you need from time well spent.

I contend that if you're complaining about something, it sometimes means you're wanting to place blame for the difficulty outside of yourself. Make sure you plan and prepare ahead so that you can make the progress you want to make. As many others have noted, by failing to prepare, you're preparing to fail.

You want to arrive at the end of each month thinking, "Wow! I accomplished this and this, and now, next month, I can . . ." If you're willing to take a hard look at yourself in the mirror around the ways you apportion your time and energy monthly, it can be empowering. You can acknowledge your ability to change your approach, skip the complaints and excuses, and truly begin to live the purposeful life you have dreamed of living.

CHAPTER 19

Weekly Progress

By now, even without looking ahead at the outline for this book, it's likely you figured that I was going to have you next think through your week. Weeks are another natural cadence for us to plan for progress. Your intent and communications are often centered on what will or could happen each week. An oft heard refrain in an office environment is, "Yep! I plan to get that done by the end of this week." And regular chitchat at the watercooler is about things that happened earlier in the week, are yet to occur in the week, or are planned for the upcoming weekend. The week is the next useful time increment by which you can structure your progress for your life on purpose.

Progress, as I'm referring to it in this book, is, pretty simply, demonstrable attention to your stated purpose that helps move you closer to your long-term vision. I think it is important to have a demonstrable way to show you've made progress each week. Then every month you will know you are on track for a meaningful quarterly calibration of your annual checkpoint.

Excitement around even long-term goals is maintained by making weekly progress. After years of enjoying our house in a cul-de-sac in Omaha, Nebraska, we made the big decision to build a house. Once the lot was selected and the plans drawn up, my wife and I went to see the progress each week, since it wasn't too far from the neighborhood we were living in at the time. We brought along expectations, admittedly sometimes unrealistic ones, for what we wanted to see completed at each visit. Some weeks, many things were completed, and we were so excited at the prospect of moving into the new home. There were other weeks, however, when quite literally not a thing happened. That was sure disappointing and frustrating because it caused us to doubt that things would ever be back on track.

Our lives are a little like that construction project. It is important for you, as you plan to live your life on purpose, to make some weekly, demonstrable progress that you can connect in some way—big or small—to your long-term vision and purpose you are pursuing. Don't let weeks go by without making positive headway.

Establish a Cadence

As you think about the ways to maximize your progress in a week, I have found it helpful to delegate Mondays as the day to set the cadence and opportunities for the week ahead. I set important meetings that day and ensure different teams and groups are in alignment on ideas and plans so that we can move forward in a way that supports the month's aims. If there is a Monday holiday, it is tough for me to get the week moving well. It could be that the previous Friday afternoon could serve as a substitute to ensure the next, short week is a solid one.

The bulk of productive activity for me happens Tuesday through Thursday. I divide my time each day to allocate time toward each of the monthly, quarterly, and annual objectives that I've set. The middle of the week is afforded for work time and meetings that require lots of thinking and energy to fast forward initiatives. These are important days to make tangible progress. If I have a personal appointment or need a day off, I try to schedule them on Friday so the focused work is not interrupted.

Friday serves as a wrap-up day for me. I finish unfinished tasks or communications. In whatever way you find works for you, find a cadence during the week that helps you feel accomplished by week's end and ready for Monday—before you exit for the weekend. For the many who work in industries that include weekend shifts and hours, your cadence will, of course, look different. Work to develop focused energy, and build in points that help you know you've made progress.

The weekend for me is reserved for faith, family, and fun and rest. On Saturdays, I spend time with my wife and children, play basketball, read, rest, or do other things that help me decompress from the week. This time is critical. I truly hope that you can carve out these important hours in your week. If you have little time for fun and rest due to work, illness, or other challenges, identify potential moments sometime during your week—even if it is not a whole day—to rest and recharge.

As I've previously noted, faith is my first priority. Sunday is reserved for time in worship and with other believers. I also share gifts and offerings with my local church. I am a big believer that a tithe of one's time, as well as earnings, is an important way to worship and serve. I typically allocate about four hours per week, where I focus on building my faith. I attend church worship services and read my Bible on my own, or other resources to help develop my capacity to teach faith-based curricula. This effort is my top priority and is the most important of my day. It serves to strengthen my foundation and enables me to make progress for my life's purpose in ways that are aligned with my top priority. For me, this is also a way to rest, so I'm well charged and ready for the next week.

As you look at your week, consider what your cadence looks like to share and maximize your time and energy around your top priorities. While some days may look repetitive, make sure you identify certain days or blocks of time such that you see your priorities well-represented in your week. You will find great satisfaction in having a week-by-week approach to living a life on purpose.

SECTION 5

Be Present on Purpose

Your journey toward living a life on purpose is well underway. You have your priorities centered. You're developing strong habits. You've crafted your purpose statement. And you've got a picture of the future—a strong vision that living your life on purpose will enable you to paint, year over year. You've set five-year milestones and begun to plan for your annual checkpoints to make sure you stay on track. You have insights on ways to calibrate your progress quarterly, and some tools to make meaningful progress each month and each week, to hold yourself accountable and ensure you're not standing still. Now, you will reflect on the importance of making the most of every day and every valuable moment.

CHAPTER 20

Daily Activity

When your months and weeks are well-ordered with allocations of your time that fit your priorities and move you toward your goals, you are free to be more deeply aware and present with each conversation and task you engage in. You want to be engaged, feeling involved and excited, rather than floating through your day. To be fully present during your day means to have your mind, energy, skills, and talents aimed toward small and big needs throughout the day. Being present means opportunities are never missed.

Being present daily starts the moment you wake. It is important to be prepared for the day each morning. By way of example, our bodies are designed to move. I struggle and feel most uncomfortable after sitting or standing for long periods of time with no movement. I travel thousands of miles a year on an airplane. I travel both domestically and internationally, with new and existing business partners, and, as I shared,

I take vision trips to spur on my growth and thinking, as well as travel for vacations with my family. I spend many hours in airports and on airplanes. As long as I'm moving between terminals or gates, or walking to pick up luggage or transportation, I feel okay, but when sitting on long flights in the same seat in the same position, my body begins to ache. Or if I'm in a long TSA line without moving, I start to shift my feet as they start to hurt.

I like to keep myself—as well as processes and projects—moving. I typically wake up prior to the alarm going off, and it doesn't seem to matter when I went to bed. I am ready for the day and ready to start work on my plan. My mind kicks into gear as I get moving in the morning, and I feel a sense of anticipation about what the day will bring. I take a look at my day and, as I get ready, I'm thinking about the conversations I need to have and what I need to do.

At breakfast, I review emails and make a mental note of who needs a follow-up. As I drive in to work, I think about conversations and emails that need to take priority, the few key points I need to share, and when I'll finish up the remaining, less critical responses or communications. Of course, my thought processes help accelerate the work once I've arrived. I feel prepared and there is order and a plan to complete the work. So, when I start, I feel focused, and the work is well directed toward the things that need to happen to ensure I make progress throughout the week.

Your habits are built through daily activities. James Clear, in his book *Atomic Habits*, reminds us that even small changes can yield big changes and outcomes over time. Early in our lives, our school schedules tend to dictate our daily activities and the weekly and monthly cadence. Our energy is largely driven by that schedule. High school is generally the first time we can begin to determine more of our daily and weekly schedule. I recall meeting with my guidance counselor as we were making my class schedule one year. I was thinking about the classes that I found hard and the ones I thought were easiest and how they fit with my study hall and P.E. class. As I was reviewing the schedule, I thought about the books I'd need, when I would head to my locker between classes, and whether I'd be sweaty from P.E. and how hungry I'd be before lunch. I didn't have a lot of choices in how my days went, but there was some, and it was good practice for life to think about how my time and energy would be spent each day.

Take Care of Yourself

Tom Rath, in his book *Eat, Move, Sleep*, is among many experts and researchers who remind us how critical it is to care for ourselves well so we can be as productive as we can be. We simply cannot be as productive in our daily activities if we do not have good health and practice healthy habits. Like others, I really need to eat to keep my energy up in the day. I try to include a fair amount of protein in my diet and stay hydrated. And yes, I need caffeine at different times in the day! Make sure you think well about how you need to fuel to bring your best energy to your days. It is not possible to be fully present, listen well, nor make the best decisions if you don't have proper nutrition. Living a life on purpose daily requires that you take care of the basics of having a strong mind and body. I have a well-stocked fridge at home and at work to help with that. I'm particularly attached to flavored water and yes, I do love the occasional Reese's peanut butter cup!

Ordered Tasks and Conversations

As I begin the workday, I hop into the key items on my mental list and the key conversations, tasks, and meetings to ensure I take steps toward weekly progress. If I have my conversations, tasks, and meetings well-ordered, I can build on ideas and work, which helps lead to more tangible results. If I begin the day without having thought through impending conversations and plans ahead of time, progress is slower.

As you consider what your daily routine looks like, think about the habits you have developed. Are the habits you have enabling you to accomplish things that help you make good weekly progress and move you toward your monthly and quarterly aims? Are you taking time for proper nutrition and hydration? Are there small shifts in your habits that you can make to help you feel and be more fully present with conversations and tasks throughout your day? Did you get the rest you needed? Did you prepare the evening or morning prior, so you can engage in tasks and meetings, ready to help team members accomplish what they need to do? It is important to start your days prepared and focused to ensure nothing distracts you from what is most important. Don't float through your days, missing out on the next great thing. Move intentionally and with purpose, developing practices and thought processes that ensure you can make progress on your weekly goals and live your life on purpose!

CHAPTER 21

Hourly Structure

Over time, I learned that it is most effective for me to engage in tasks in hourly blocks of time. If I have a meeting that is longer than one hour, it becomes more difficult to maintain interest and energy. While it varies for everyone, this time block aligns with neuropsychology research that suggests adults, on average, can maintain focus from ten to fifty-two minutes at a time.[9] Sometimes I can feel overwhelmed by the amount of information or not be able to recall details from the conversation. This isn't only true at work, but in my personal life as well. Therefore, I think carefully about maintaining an hourly approach to structuring my day. It is the way I manage my capacity and help ensure that my energy and time are managed optimally. You might find that

9   "Focus on Concentration," Harvard Medical School, *Harvard Health Publishing* (blog), February 1, 2020, https://www.health.harvard.edu/mind-and-mood/focus-on-concentration.

you need time to work in to being fully focused or your thoughts need more time to engage, so perhaps the hourly structure needs adjusting for you, but do think about the amount of time you spend on any given meeting or task. Build in the proverbial "brain break" if the task you are doing requires many long hours to complete. Some research indicates that including some physical movement during that brain break is helpful. Decide if that is one hour or longer but pay attention to the effectiveness of your time spent, and how many minutes you are able to work at your highest level of thinking and productivity.

When E4 and I built the tiny house together, I put the plans together, ordered the supplies, and managed a project plan in hourly blocks of time. It helped to keep the project moving along during the increments of time we were able to spend doing it. Of course, I'd never built a tiny house before, so I set goals for the timeframe to complete the tasks. I began with just a rough estimate of what it would take, for example, to lay the subfloor—the first step in building the tiny house.

I bought a trailer for the tiny house that already had steel floor joists, so I measured and determined how much wood I needed to order for the subfloor. When I began to lay the subfloor, I determined how much space I covered in the first ten minutes, and from there, esti-mated how much time I needed to cover the entire 450-square-foot space with the subfloor. After I put down the first ten screws, I knew that I had greatly underestimated the time that it would take to finish this first part of the project. My estimations were off initially because till then, I'd only drilled screws into wood. I had never worked with a steel frame when drilling screws before. It took so much more effort. With the steel frame, I needed to use self-tapping screws, which took much more pressure, power from the drill, and generally, more time to get all the way into the frame.

I let Dana know what piece of the project we were working on before we headed off each evening. I was running out of time one night as I was working on the flooring, so I needed to clean up the jobsite and prepare to finish the floor during the next building session. I laid out the sheets in the proper area, set the drill to charge up, and measured the remaining area so I could compute the time needed to complete that floor next time. When I returned home, I had just the right amount of time to shower and head to bed. The process felt long, and I was concerned about my slow progress. But as I love thinking about things in hourly structured increments, I kept working on those screws, measuring distance between each one, and figuring out how many I could do with a single battery charge of the drill. Then I figured out how much time each square foot of subfloor was going to take. I got better at it, of course, so I could pick up the pace just a bit, and my estimation of the total time needed for the project became more precise. Needless to say, again, it certainly took longer than I thought it would before realizing all of the required effort, but I adjusted and worked on my hourly schedule to finish the tasks.

Tracking Your Time

Your hours are important. You've likely been to hour-long meetings where exactly zero things were accomplished. And, at least I hope, you've been in hour-long meetings where much was accomplished. To increase the chances of having an hour well spent requires a strong plan of how to structure the meeting and what you really hope to accomplish by the conclusion of it.

In the same way that I evaluated my subflooring project for my tiny-house build, it is good to assess the time and intent for each hour or meeting. In the first few minutes, assess how the conversation can progress toward best outcomes. Once you have that determined, consider the details that need to be accomplished, what tools you need, and what might hold you back. In the second half of the hour, identify any knowledge gaps, identify solutions (if appropriate), and always be sure to summarize—and assign—next steps. If you miss that last step, you will have a tough time making the weekly progress you want to make.

Again, I realize you likely plan meetings or projects similarly, by the hour or perhaps another increment. However, it's important to bring a strong structure and plan to what you hope to accomplish. It is easy to see an hour of time pass with little movement or progress. Having productive hours is not only important for you, but also for others. A fast way to get people to stop spending time with you or to cease tapping you as a resource is to waste their time. Time is valuable and it feels bad, of course, to have it wasted. If you are waiting an inordinate amount of time to see a medical professional, you'll decide if their expertise is worth that wait, or you will simply find another doctor. As consumers of any service, we expect to have our time respected, so it is important to demonstrate for others that respect that we expect for ourselves. When you bring a structure and plan to the hour, you build trust instead of eroding it.

Consider what you are doing to ensure that your hours are well-structured. Look to see whether you have appropriately scheduled your most challenging tasks during your most productive hours. Have a process for ensuring that one-hour meetings or other tasks are well planned ahead of time. A rule of thumb for ensuring your meetings/activities are on track is to start the hour by quickly reviewing the topic or topics to be covered, naming the objectives for the meeting, doing the core tasks and/or engaging in the core conversations, decision-making (if appropriate), and identifying and assigning follow-up steps. A life on purpose happens over time, but it also happens in daily and hourly increments of time.

CHAPTER 22

Transformational
Meetings

Because so much of our time and days involve meetings with others, it merits including additional perspective on ways to make your meetings not just productive—but truly transformative experiences for you and others. You will often live out your purpose in the presence of other people. Our schedules and structure become personal as we interact and work with others.

Meetings are not productive if they are not prepared well. Preparation helps drive productivity. A common misstep in structuring hours during the day is forgetting how critical it is to block the hours needed to prepare for meetings. Preparation is not only about the topics and items that need to be addressed in the meeting, but also, most importantly, about the people.

As mentioned, start with the objective of the meeting—what the intended outcome is. Your life on purpose requires both focus and preparation to ensure you don't remain stagnant and that your time is maximized toward achieving your goals. Your meetings, your minutes, and your moments are all valuable components to having productive hours, days, weeks, etc. The best meetings become avenues for your progress, and the outcomes may be transformative, but only when you prepare well ahead of time.

Effective meetings are marked by effective communication. There are (at least) four different kinds of content that are shared during meetings: things we want people to know about us, things we think they want to know generally, what we know they need to hear or learn, and information that will help them leave transformed. The more that people leave a meeting feeling like the communication they participated in was transformational, the more likely we experience our life on purpose. It is worth it to aim for this transformational kind of communication and moment in a meeting. Ideally, people will leave the meeting inspired. You should leave more ready to fulfill your purpose statement.

In conversations, people communicate things they want others to know about themselves. Social media is filled with this kind of content. They post about their celebrations, much less frequently about struggles, or even mundane things like what they wore or ate that day. The information and content is shared with hopes of helping the consumers of the content get to know us better, and posts are generally designed to show ourselves in a positive light. This same thing happens in conversation, as people tell many details about themselves and their experiences or frustrations. We have all been part of conversations during which the other person spends an inordinate amount of time talking about themselves. I'd submit that, generally, this kind of conversation rarely has any transformational elements, though it could support some relational connection.

Sometimes conversations involve sharing information we want others to know. This is sometimes more interesting if it is information that is particularly relevant to the hearer's experiences or needs. We swap recipes or favorite restaurant experiences, or talk about sports teams we follow or ideas about a historical, political, or social topic. These conversations can also help deepen relational connections, and even if there is some disagreement, this type of conversation can build interest and energy if there is common interest in the topics discussed.

Another kind of conversation involves communicating things that are explicitly designed to meet the preference and need of the audience. This deeper level of communication involves listening well to learn about the other person, employing empathy and concern, especially if the information we're conveying is particularly meaningful or has an impact on their life in greater ways beyond general interest in a topic. Sometimes this kind of conversation, depending upon the context, might be directive, such as instructing your teen not to speed through the neighborhood. It might be another level of instruction that supports personal growth or development, such as a coach or teacher providing guidance designed to help an individual improve their performance on the field or in the classroom. There has been much work done in this space that suggests instruction and direction that leads to growth and change is generally best shared within the context of a trusting relationship.

There is yet an even deeper, more meaningful level of conversation that warrants preparation and intentionality and that can yield transformative outcomes when done thoughtfully. Transformational conversations result in positive changes in our mindset as well as our behavior and could ultimately lead to more fulfilling lives. These seminal conversations transform the ways we think, feel, and act, and are often memorable and mark pivotal moments that provide a vantage point to gauge what life was like before and after that interaction. While sometimes those types of communications occur by happenstance, they can be intentionally planned, and, as you grow as a leader, you can begin to work on what elements are required to prepare for a conversation to ensure it is most effective and has transformative results for yourself and others.

How to Prepare for Transformation

This book project is a direct result of such a transformative meeting for me. In high school, I was attending a faith-based group, and our leader made an effort to invest in my personal growth. After one of our events, he asked if I had some time to meet with him during the week, and I agreed to meet up for lunch at a local restaurant. He told me that he had been observing my talents and interactions over the previous weeks and months and noticed that I had the capacity to influence my peers. He let me know he appreciated my communication and care for others, and that other people liked being around me. He encouraged me to think carefully about what I was doing with that capacity to influence others.

I had not thought a lot about that before. We talked for a while, and he challenged me to think about my purpose and then asked if I was willing to serve in a leadership role for the group. I agreed, and I appreciate that he didn't just leave it at that. He worked to help me understand principles of leadership. We met weekly to help build leadership skills that I could use to serve our group better. I realized that my perceptions of myself shifted at that point. Instead of just having fun trying to convince someone to support my ideas, I felt more responsible for the ways I influenced others and wanted to be more purposeful about it. I'm glad that I had such a transformative conversation when I was young so that I understood early that influence is something to be wielded with care and consideration for others. That it ought to be used in others' best interest rather than for my own. I believe this yet today and strive to live by those principles.

As I reflected on that meeting, I thought about what made it transformational. I know that the leader who initiated the conversation had reflected and prepared well for our conversation. He was specific about his observations and was clear and forthcoming about the objective: to identify and enhance my capacity as a leader and provide a chance for me to practice leadership. He shared what he had seen in the past, contextualized it to the present circumstances for our group, and provided a picture of an aspirational future state. At the time, he painted a vision that was unclear to me, but which I now understand is what I wanted and was created to do. It was such a pivotal meeting because he was prepared and clearly communicated, and it was a transformational experience for me.

For each meeting you have, consider who is attending, why they are there, and what it would take to have them leave transformed. Picture their faces, voices, spheres of influence, priorities, stages of life, and directions they are headed. I consider the barriers they might be facing in fulfilling their purpose, since again, this is the approach I take to help propel leaders. Consider the words and language you will use at the meeting and the sequence of the points you want to communicate to ensure that the content is shared in an empathetic and transformational way.

To be transformational, first, do your homework. Share things you have learned and observed. People appreciate it when others notice well. Then, remain focused on the best possible outcomes. It is important that others leave the meeting feeling supported and valued rather than defensive, which rarely leads to change. Help the hearers know what you see and the possibilities for a better outcome and future ahead. It is important to describe that envisioned future. Next, figure out steps and processes to achieving those possibilities moving forward.

CHAPTER 23

Make the Most of Your Minutes

There are, of course, sixty minutes in an hour and one thousand four hundred forty total minutes in one day. And, as Oliver Burkeman reminds us in his book *Four Thousand Weeks*, if you live till you are eighty years old, you have a total of about twenty-eight million waking minutes available in your lifetime. These sound like big numbers, which is deceiving. It is too easy to undervalue those precious minutes. If you're not careful, your purposeful life can be stymied by wasted, unaccounted-for minutes. Life is absurdly short. Do not let minutes sneak past you wasted and rendered useless on the cutting room floor of your life with no story, no connections, and no lasting or purposeful thing to show for them.

Sometimes all you have is a few precious minutes of interaction with others, and often those minutes can be maximized during the waiting we do so often. Those minutes do not always need to be idle, but rather, they may be unanticipated opportunities for connection with others. You must learn to recognize that minutes you have are not haphazard but instead could be like finding the proverbial pearl in an oyster. They could be a small treasure where you can create connection and be more purposeful.

When our kids became more involved in activities and sports, I was always grateful for those few minutes in the drive to practice to connect with them. Like many families, as the kids grew, our lives got busier and more scheduled, and lots more minutes were suddenly accounted for, so that driving time became so valuable. I asked their thoughts about faith, family, school, and their interests, and I shared principles and values that I hoped that they would learn to adopt in their lives. Sometimes the radio was turned down for our conversations, and sometimes it was turned up, so we could loudly sing together—occasionally even on key. Those times to practice in the car were amazing minutes for connection. Sometimes they were in the mood for those conversations, and of course, sometimes not as much, but I sure relished that time with them.

When the kids were older, we started to carpool with other families. It was a great time to make connections with other families and my kids' friends. Of course, each family is very different, but it was a privilege to be another caring adult for a young person. I asked our carpool mates similar questions and listened to their answers. Those connections were also special. It was a privilege to speak to kids at such a pivotal point in their young lives and share some hope or direction as they struggled with their faith, their sports careers, or other challenges they faced. It is not possible to know the outcome for each of the meetings and minutes we share with others or to what extent they are transformational. But it was a privilege to sow those seeds of hope for the future. Even years later, if I happened to run into one of those kids at a restaurant, event, or even graduation parties, they would approach and chat with me because those connections were so special and long-lasting.

Take Every Opportunity to Connect

Be ready to capitalize on every minute you have to connect with others. Take a moment to consider who is with you in those minutes. Those connections can happen with friends and even strangers, at the grocery store, at the airport, or at school events. Some are more adept at reading nonverbal language and can be ready to share care or empathy if something is difficult, and others find it easy to engage in conversation. Lean on your strengths and your personal purpose to know the best ways to capitalize on the minutes you have and the connections you can make.

Seize the moment at hand to provide encouragement to someone who needs it. Your purpose should be in action in the long term, and you can live your purpose each minute as you adopt a posture that considers others' needs. My purpose includes being ready to have "intuitive interaction"—which simply means noticing and assessing what people might need and then figuring out how I might assist.

A few intentional minutes of asking or listening might be a game-changer for someone who needs an encouraging word. Loneliness remains a concern, even though we are more digitally connected as a society than ever before. I think making connections that are meaningful requires something more than just a virtual platform.

Traveling globally, I quickly learned that electrical power is available, of course, in most places. However, you cannot connect your devices to that power because the outlet shapes and voltage compatibility are different than they are for standard outlets in your home country. You must be prepared with appropriate plug adapters that allow you to connect to the energy source where you are. Similarly, when we attempt to make connections with people, sometimes it is easier to make a connection with others in an environment that is familiar to us or where we share many things in common, but if you are somewhere more unfamiliar or there are many cultural and societal differences, we might need to be more prepared to connect in meaningful or productive ways.

I appreciate the connections that I get to make with people who might be experiencing a barrier in their life that prevents them from fully living their life on purpose, and humor can be a quick way to connect. Laughter and happiness bring positive energy and are a good bridge builder. The *World Happiness Report* is a collaborative effort to measure happiness by nation-states. It advocates for the importance of happiness—alongside standard measures of a nation's success, such as job growth, GDP, or population statistics—to understand the level of well-being of a nation's people. It may be a small thing, but using humor, for me, is a small way to infuse some happiness, build some trust, make a connection, and learn a bit about ways I can help those who might appreciate or need it. It is a good posture to then bring a little bit of hope for the future. Like many dads, I appreciate good—or even a few bad—puns, self-deprecating humor, or just find the funniness in circumstances that can help open opportunities for other conversation.

Helping someone smile or laugh is perhaps a small window of opportunity. But for me, it's a reminder that people remember how you made them feel, even if they forget exactly what you said. So, sharing some fun and laughter is a worthwhile way to spend a minute, brightening up someone else's day. It's tough, as I pursue my own life on purpose, to propel someone to overcome barriers if I haven't taken a minute to connect with them and share a positive moment. Humor is a little avenue for beginning that more involved journey.

As you think about your life, the conversations you have each day, can you identify where there are minutes wasted and not maximized so you can more intentionally live your life on purpose? You might have chances to share meaningful minutes between meetings, at that watercooler, or even as you see servers from your favorite restaurants and shops. Stop wasting those minutes and start using them for brief but potentially impactful connections.

Be thoughtful about the ways you initiate connections in those few minutes you have in a day. While not everyone can be as funny as me, you can connect in ways that honor your abilities and interests. Live your life on purpose in small and big ways, starting with minutes where you make the most of the connections you make with others. You can start doing that today!

CHAPTER 24

Attentional Moments

Living your life on purpose starts with singular moments. Those moments when you pay close attention and fully appreciate the opportunities they represent. Intentionality in these moments can result in transformational, more purposeful minutes, meetings, days, years, and lives. Moments are not only those brief experiences that occur in the regular course of a day or just by happenstance, but they are also those meaningful events in our lives—and in the lives of those that we care about—that leave lasting, core memories, and have the potential to inspire us for the future. These are the things you can't miss, and which might often mark a new beginning—a small or a significant new life chapter. Interestingly, the most important moments often mark the end of something, making room for the new chapter to begin—the critical moment that signals something new is about to start. High school graduation marks the end of compulsory education and the beginning of postsecondary education or a vocation. When a child is born, it marks the end of pregnancy and prenatal experiences and the start of postnatal experiences and parenthood. A wedding marks the end of engagement and the beginning, of course, of marriage and a new course in life. There are countless examples where a moment—or event—in our lives signals a change that launches us into new possibilities.

Soon after I was married, I began teaching a Bible study for a small group of newly married couples. It occurred to me as we had different conversations about God and life how much focus, anticipation, and planning had been centered around the wedding, but how little thinking had been dedicated to the future that moment represented. The potential bound up at the moment of marriage hadn't yet been realized. The life purpose they had as individuals and as couples did not garner nearly as much time and focus.

Moments That Matter

In observing the tendency of people to spend their energy involved in the celebration itself, rather than sharing time and energy considering the opportunities that the moment initiates, I resolved to have more attentional moments and to encourage others to have them as well. In short, being attentional with your moments means exactly what it sounds like, paying close attention and turning your mind toward the moment to consider how it facilitates your life on purpose. An attentional moment leads you to embrace all that the moment means for now and for the future.

As I process attentional moments, I think about each of the people present and what they have contributed and will contribute to the celebration itself and to the realization of the win, goal reached, or next step or phase. Of course, I strive to be attentional, not only during big moments, changes, or celebrations, but I also bring that mindset to the daily moments as well.

I was once at a family wedding, and I noticed a sibling of the bride. I had known this person for their entire life, and they seemed to be feeling nervous and maybe a little uncomfortable. In that moment, I wanted to provide some peace and assurance, so I let them know that I noticed the energy and time they were contributing to the day in their role and told them I believed that they were going to positively change lives in their future. I helped them know their care and disposition was making a positive difference not only in the life of their sibling, but also in others' lives. It was a brief moment in a long day, but I think I helped them feel a little more relaxed and confident. Many years later, I had a chance to spend a little more time with them, and it was clear that they had reached a better place in life than where they'd been the day of that wedding. It seemed that they believed the future they hoped for was achievable—and worth fighting for. While I am sure that moment we encountered was not the only element that helped steer them toward the better place, I hope it served as a little wind in their sail.

I have dear friends who lost two of their children—ages ten and sixteen years old—in a heartbreaking automobile accident that forever changed their lives. When I spoke to the husband, he wished that he could know why it happened. He also wanted others to find hope in faith in Jesus Christ.

After I had that conversation, I took my seat before the memorial service began. There were many students there who were struggling. I joined a small huddle with my own kids and a few others and prayed with them. I don't recall the exact words, but I wanted to share hope with them and that they would find some peace through faith in God through Jesus Christ.

Sometime following that day, the mother who lost her children contacted me and asked me about a photo that she saw on the anniversary of the funeral. She wanted to know who was in the huddle and what I had shared and prayed with them. I looked at the photo, and I shared that one of the boys in the photo, who was now a young man, had become a Christian around that time. He now serves as an intern at a church and actively shares his faith with others. He also shared his faith with his younger brother, who has an active faith himself. The younger brother was not at the funeral that day and was just twelve years old at the time. He is now friends with one of the siblings who survived the crash that day, and they serve and are growing in their faith together.

I'm thankful I could reflect a bit about that moment with those students to share some of what happened to encourage the life and faith of the young people who were there. I believe God is always working, even in the most difficult moments, to call people to Himself and His hope in Christ.

Consider whether there are moments—big or small—that you have let pass by without engaging with more attention and purpose. At your next opportunity, turn your mind to consider the individuals in the room and what they might need. Notice those who might not be noticed by someone else. If there is something you can say or do in that moment that aligns with your purpose, do not let that moment pass by without taking that small or big action. You cannot know the impact it might have.

Living your life on purpose begins with moments. Transformation can be initiated with a careful, intentional moment. While big moments like commencement, marriages, new job first days, even funerals, have endings associated with them—some frightening and others celebratory—each of them marks a moment for possibility and a new direction. When you are attentional in the moment, you can live your life on purpose, and be the catalyst for transformation. Go be purposeful and begin to transform the world through your legacy.

A Legacy of Purpose

L iving your life on purpose is about realizing you have only one life to live and one life to share. You need to make the most of it. In previous sections of the book, you identified your priorities, developed habits that help you to honor those priorities, crafted your unique life purpose, and learned ways to practice fulfilling your purpose year by year and moment by moment. Now, you will learn ways to build a strong legacy, as you faithfully fulfill your purpose in life.

CHAPTER 25

Invest in Others

Most people associate legacy with how they will be remembered. They think about the things people will think and say about them after they are gone, salient memories they have of the individual, and sometimes possessions or items they leave behind that had value or remind them of their life and work. While these are important elements of remembering, these are more a result of the role that individual had in our lives—father, friend, or coworker. These memories are very important and valuable.

But leaving a legacy also includes leaving a legacy of purpose that leaves an indelible mark on the lives of those we touch throughout our lifetimes. A legacy of purpose leads to transformed lives. When people we spend time with are transformed by our lives, it can create a legacy that transcends time. A purposeful legacy is additive to memory-making and is built through the relational fabric of our lives. Our words and actions not only are heard and observed but also lead to others' lives being changed for good.

A purposeful legacy requires your time. It is why I spent so much time considering long-term and short-range perspectives on how to be intentional with your time. We spend time with people in celebratory moments and in moments of disappointment and heartache. We share our time, talents, and energy during minutes, meetings, days, weeks, months, and years to convey our principles and values in a way that helps people see a more positive future for themselves.

Finding the Potential in Others

Over the years, I've had a propensity for supporting young, college-aged adults. It's such a critical transition time in life as they are making decisions about who they are and who they want to be. They are making decisions about post-secondary education and vocation options, while also—either consciously or maybe subconsciously—determining what elements of their upbringing, habits, and viewpoints they've heard will become their own as they become independent young adults. They might choose a profession that a family member is in or choose a different direction. They might elect to remain in their hometown for school or work, or to journey far from the place where they were raised. It is a good opportunity to help young people begin to identify and pursue their priorities and discover how they want to spend their lives on purpose.

When I graduated college and was seeking my first full-time job, I was not necessarily seeking the highest-paying job, nor was I looking for a job in a particular location, nor even a particular role. I was looking for a company that was willing to invest in me as a person and professional. I wanted to make a contribution, to provide value, and also be part of a place that would help me build my skills and talents.

Early jobs I had taught me about marketing, customer service, sales, management, and organizational structure. I learned about financial management, the function of technology, and personal development. I learned the value and role of shareholders, company leaders, and the impact of politics and statutes on business. Again, these learnings are still applicable, and I appreciate them to this day. But even beyond each of these critical elements of running a successful business, I began to appreciate the value of creating a legacy built on living a life on purpose every day.

Having an orientation toward leaving a legacy built on making values-based choices, rather than position, title, or even pay, will ensure that you are moving in a direction that will provide you with peace and a sense of fulfillment as your purpose becomes apparent to others and they see your choices and are positively influenced by them.

While there are likely innumerable people with whom you could share your time and energy with as you live your life on purpose, it is important to focus on those you have the best opportunity to influence. I mentioned that my purpose statement says I will "propel leaders," so I am always on the lookout for those with leadership potential and capacity. And because I have chances to intersect with college students, whether it is at my kids' university or at a sports or faith-based event, I tend to seek students that demonstrate leadership abilities that are promising, though sometimes not yet refined. I watch for their energy, commitment, character, and discipline, and, especially, for the ways they treat others. Sometimes, I'll have a conversation that involves inviting them to consider an internship at my company or suggest other opportunities where they might have a chance to learn and grow.

Investing Wisely

As previously described, I aim for conversations to be transformational, in that I'm looking for ways to connect them to an opportunity that will resonate with them over time. Upon finding the right connection and opportunity, I observe and monitor their growth and progress. Unlike Ron Popeil's famous advertising mantra, a purposeful legacy is not built on a "Set it and forget it!" mindset. It requires tracking and gauging, just like managing our long-term financial investments requires; creating a legacy should not be left to chance. Jesus told a power parable about a rich young ruler who allocated talents—an apportion of resources in different amounts—ten for one, five for the next, and one for the last one. While those entrusted with ten talents and five talents each invested and magnified those resources, the third buried their one talent in the hopes of protecting it but experienced no return on that investment. Frustrated, the ruler pulled that single talent to entrust to the one who had invested and experienced the most return.

It is easy to miss some of the important messages of the parable. Many people are inclined to be like the one who buried his one talent. We tend to bury those talents and never use and apply them to see what might come of them. You have *so* much to give and offer, and the returns—not simply in financial terms but in terms of relational growth, wellness for yourself and others, and healthier workplaces, communities, and organizations—would be exponentially better if each individual committed to understanding and using each of their own internal—not just external—investments to build a purposeful legacy that yields more good in the world. Additionally, the rich ruler clearly had a purpose in mind in allocating and apportioning those investments. He wanted his people to be courageous and faithful with what he had entrusted them with. He knew how valuable those talents were but that the potential for those talents was contingent on the intent of the one who was stewarding them. He didn't need to take the coins back for himself, instead he gave another opportunity for the one to be invested properly.

Understand that not everyone you hope to support or share and invest your time and energy in will receive and use that investment in the same manner or to the same extent. That is okay! Your role is to be consistent in finding a right way and right space and, if applicable, a right person to share your time, talent, and sometimes even your treasure with, in the hope that it will build a legacy in return—not only for you but, most importantly, for them.

Consider your circle of influence. Write down names and the ways that you currently connect with different people. Think about groups that you think your purpose aligns with best. Do you have particular care and interest in sharing your purpose with them? For some of you, your purpose statement is very clear and will more easily point you in the direction you should go to begin legacy building—one transformational connection at a time. For others, your purpose could be lived out in many ways or with many people, but again, your time and energy are finite, so be specific as you think about who you want to begin supporting as you live out your purpose. Be intentional about your communication and discern what is needed from the individual and from yourself as you consider potential next steps.

CHAPTER 26

Align to Grow

Another way to build a legacy as you live your life on purpose is to make connections with people who align with you. They may be living in a similar life stage, have similar roles and responsibilities, or have a shared vantage point. They may align with your hopes, beliefs, or ideas. You might have a shared passion, and they bring different experiences that help deepen your understanding or broaden your vision for the future. These unique relationships help each person grow and develop as you envision possibilities and work together. It is energizing to pursue your purpose and build your legacy alongside others who may be rowing in the same direction in life.

I tend to intentionally seek out those I align with. I review their social media, or if they have a public presence, I review their books or other content, and work on having a chance to meet and share some time. Formally and informally, finding times where we can challenge and encourage development as "iron sharpens iron" takes some effort. Review your calendar, as previous chapters discuss, to find time to connect with those who can enable you to live your life on purpose and build your legacy, and for whom you can do the same.

In any sport or game that I compete in, I always look for someone better than me to practice with and compete against. Some people enjoy sports as recreation, or they enjoy playing for the easy win. They have fun playing the game and may, or may not, break a sweat playing it. This is not me. I always bring intensity and want to give 100 percent because whether I win or lose, I want to improve. I think people see me as highly competitive. That is probably true, but it's also not that simple. I think developmentally. My focus is always on getting better, again, whether I am winning or losing the game. I'd rather lose but improve my skills than win easily and regress in my abilities. It is tempting in any area of our lives to remain entirely focused on the outcome—i.e., winning the game—but miss out on the developmental opportunity. The development and growth that occur are eternal.

Mindfully Aligning

As you spend time with individuals with whom you feel aligned, figure out what you want to focus on. I once read the book *One Perfect Word* in which Debbie Macomber encourages readers to focus on one word for a whole year and develop that thing in their lives. It is a simple approach that I liked. My word was "purpose." I wrote my purpose statement, became even more clear about my purpose in life, and wrote this book about purpose. Since you've read this far in the book, you might think, "This guy is one of the more passionate people about purpose that I've come across!" That may be true, but sometimes we can get comfortable and miss the chance to develop and grow if we are passionate about something, or practice and focus on it for a while. But there is always more to learn and ways to grow. I needed to find and align with someone who was even more passionate and focused on purpose than I was, to help me become even more capable of pursuing and understanding it. I don't want to miss out on the chance to build my skills and capacity in this arena.

If you determine the area you want to grow and develop, figure out the voices and authors you might read and listen to. As I mentioned, I've read and perused dozens of books about purpose and studied leaders who lived out their purpose intently. I think it is a lot of fun to study their thoughts, words, actions, practices, and the ways they persevered. I consider different authors' voices and ways their perspectives align or contrast with one another and with my own. It challenges and grows my thinking. You may not enjoy reading books as much as I do, but figure out the ways you can interact with others' voices to grow and challenge your thinking.

I had conversations about purpose with colleagues, friends, and others, sharing references from readings and asking their thoughts around specific topics. I wanted to figure out ways that our perspectives aligned or contrasted, field test my own thoughts, and stretch my thinking. If there was a way we could more concretely work together on an idea or project, I suggested it, if there was a right opportunity. It is exciting and fulfilling to connect with those who are excited about developing and growing throughout their lives. I've met leaders, parents, volunteers, and others who are intent on growing. To build a legacy, it is imperative that you find ways to continue learning and finding others who can support your development. Otherwise, your growth gets stuck, and you might repeat one year's experiences for the next twenty.

Sometimes people you've previously aligned with become misaligned—your interests or circumstances change, you grow at different rates, perspectives shift, or life choices are much different. You might decide you need to exit that relationship. Change is always difficult and particularly so when it involves relationships. You might question yourself and your purpose, reflect on the conversations and experiences you shared, wondering why the shift and change is happening, and feel unsure about how to proceed. I encourage you to be faithful to pursue your purpose and find others who can align with you, encourage you, and continue helping you grow.

Again, your energy and your time are finite. Spend that energy enriching relationships with those who are eager and able to support you as you live your life on purpose, so you can continue to grow and build a legacy. In reality survival shows, people are always working to figure out what is needed to endure another day. The survivalist wants to be prepared and might initially load up their backpack in preparation for the journey, but inevitably, it gets too heavy. Then the skilled survivalist who wants to win must sort out what is most essential and get the load down to a manageable amount.

The survivor knows that if you are weighed down, it will keep you from moving forward, and there is only so much energy they can rely on in their own body to make it to the end of the race. You might feel like you are carrying a heavy backpack and feel burdened by a relationship that has caused discouragement, that has changed and is stopping you from pursuing your purpose, or that is preventing you from reaching your hoped-for destination. But you carry with you the growth, lessons, and learnings from that relationship as you march toward your purpose. Those lessons have great value as you pursue your highest priorities, live your life on purpose, and build a legacy.

Reflect on your life and think about those that you align with and those who might be able to help you grow in areas that will help you live your life on purpose even more intentionally and capably. Consider ways you might support and encourage them in the same way. Also, reflect on relationships that feel burdensome and are making it difficult for you to focus on your priorities and pursue your purpose.

I challenge you to live a life on purpose with people who are aligned with you and with whom you can mutually develop and grow. It is a critical element of building a legacy in your life that results in transformation for others.

CHAPTER 27

Authentically Mentor

We all gain knowledge and experience as we journey through life. You sometimes hear people say that they have forgotten more than younger people know. But too often, people do not take time to share their learnings with those who might benefit, and those decades of accumulated experiences and learnings are not ever shared and passed along to someone else. A life on purpose lends itself to mentoring others. Maybe you don't yet see yourself as a potential mentor. However, as you age and have more years behind you than ahead of you, I urge you to see the imperative for mentoring someone from the next generation who will carry the torch of building a positive legacy in a new way.

I often share my approach for living a life on purpose by decade. I believe that in your twenties you should try everything. In your thirties, pick something. In your forties, master what you've selected. In your fifties, mentor others with what you've mastered, and in your sixties, transition that mastery.

For many young adults in their twenties, it can be difficult to home in on a single purpose because they simply have not yet developed enough perspective to decide. People often ask new high school graduates and college-aged students what they are studying and what they want to do when they graduate. They haven't had enough experience to respond and may lack perspective on the kinds of contexts where they might work and thrive. Studies vary, but at least one-third of college graduates are not employed in a field related to their college major. But, in your twenties, you may have more ideas, energy, and gumption! Thoughts are yet forming, and you are willing to learn and try new things. Some are more open to feedback and advice. It is good advice for everyone— but especially as you are figuring out a future purpose for your life—to tamp down pride, refuse to dig your heels in, and be willing to accept feedback to help you learn, change, and grow to set yourself up for success. Try things in all areas of the priorities you've committed to—faith, family, work, and recreation and rest—or another priority area. Each experience, each activity, every commitment, is a potential teacher with lessons that can be lifelong. In your twenties, go ahead, try new things through work, clubs, your faith community, volunteering, or other ways to explore and decide the kinds of things you could do to pursue your life on purpose.

In our thirties, it is time to settle on something to pursue. Our purpose will be refined during this span of time. Sometimes our family lives have changed but settled, we've chosen a location we prefer to live in for a while, and our preferences have become more defined. By this time, we've had some experiences to inform what we like or want to do and more clarity around what we don't. It is the right time to pick something to focus on. It is the right time to solidify a purpose statement, ensuring it has elements that are eternal (for your whole life), transcendent (reach beyond you), and universal (applicable for each area of your life). Craft the purpose statement word-by-word, refining it so that you feel confident that you can build a legacy around it and have a transformational impact on those you choose to invest in and develop along the way.

As you enter midlife in your forties, you will develop a level of mastery as you pursue your purpose. Hopefully, you've worked diligently throughout the days, weeks, months, quarters, and many years of practice and development in areas that helped you to live your life on purpose. You might even see your long-range vision beginning to take shape, and you can apply your energy even more carefully and intentionally. As you continue to persevere, there will be moments where you realize you've developed mastery around your talents, skills, and practices aimed at fulfilling your life on purpose. Others may begin to seek your advice or offer admiration as you are generous with your time and energy, building a legacy that transforms those around you.

In your fifties, you can begin to reflect on your decades of effort and purposeful living. You notice those in their twenties and thirties figuring out and refining their purpose. You might consider mentoring one of them, investing in their life on purpose to ensure members of the next generation realize they have so much to give, helping them understand there are so many transformational connections they can make to realize a powerful long-term vision for their own life and legacy.

Enriching Others

A mentor, of course, shares their knowledge and experience to support and coach another individual toward a better future in one or more areas. Mentoring might include sharing practical information, but it is more about helping an individual believe in and grow their talent, character, soft skills, or habits to help them fulfill their own purpose. You might help them continue to define and honor their priorities and encourage them in ways they are sharing their finite time and energy.

Mentors who really change lives are able to help their mentees adopt mindsets that lead to positive thoughts, words, and actions. They serve as sounding boards to identify barriers to creating and fulfilling a long-term vision. Perhaps you are early in your own journey to live your life on purpose, so it is difficult to envision taking on a mentoring role. But even now, consider the ways you want to lead people to live out their values and coach them when they are feeling stuck and are not seeing hoped-for results. It is a true privilege to come alongside someone in their journey.

Mentoring requires commitment to others' growth, time, and empathy. Each mentor-mentee match will be different in what it might require of you, and everyone's capacity is different. But be transparent about your intent, availability, and capacity as a mentor and ask and listen about the expectations and hopes for the mentee. Identify a period of time and meeting cadence for the mentoring relationship, then review the progress and content of your conversations and determine if it makes sense to continue or adjust going forward. I recommend mentoring no more than a few people at a time. I've tended to reference a biblical framework for mentoring approaches, in that Jesus had twelve disciples during his ministry, and there are several references to three of those disciples serving as a trusted circle. He certainly was a teacher, modeling ways to live in relationship with God and others, and helping his disciples understand the reasons for setting and honoring priorities and growing healthy and purposeful lives.

Many successful people acknowledge their experienced mentors who helped them to reach the pinnacle of their field. Their mentors helped them focus on the right priorities and habits needed to grow and succeed.

John Wooden was one of the greatest college basketball coaches of all time. Some might say he was one of the greatest coaches in any sport. He won an unprecedented ten NCAA national championships in twelve years as the coach of the UCLA Bruins. At one point during his nearly thirty-year career, 1948 to 1975, his teams had an eighty-eight-game winning streak. He was awarded National Coach of the Year seven times. Beyond his incredible winning record, many of his players acknowledge the profound impact Wooden had on them as players and as people. He was available to his players off the court as well as on, and they credit him with support in their personal growth. While the game changed, the principles that Wooden taught are timeless. It is our role as mentors to encourage mentees to adopt principles that are timeless. John Wooden left a legacy not only because of his exemplary skills, first playing and then coaching the game of basketball, but also because he encouraged the personal growth in his players, staff, and others. He espoused strong values and character built on love, integrity, and self-discipline. He wanted his players to know that as you focus on these and other aspects of your personal character, a strong reputation with others will follow.

If you are in your twenties and thirties, and you do not have a mentor, begin to think about your circle of friends and acquaintances. Consider who might align with your purpose and has knowledge and experiences that could support your growth. Think about what you need or would hope to learn from a mentor. Then reach out to those individuals who have priorities, character, and/or habits that you would like to learn to adopt and emulate. Contact them and ask if they would consider a mentoring role for a period of time. Many people will feel honored to be asked, even if they are not able to do it. If you are someone who has some life experiences under your belt, think about mentoring someone younger and be ready to share the experiences, values, learnings, and habits you've developed over time. Your life on purpose is a lifelong pursuit. As the race progresses, you should not slow down, but you should pick up the pace and finish strong in the end.

CHAPTER 28

Sprint through the Finish

Everyone loves a good ending. In entertainment, whether it is a sports event, a movie, or a book, we all appreciate a memorable, emotional, intense ending. We want to feel a connection with the people or the characters to feel like we are a part of something significant. It is part of why we cheer for an athlete or are loyal fans of a sports team. We can feel personally invested in the outcome and, of course, we want that outcome to be a happily-ever-after kind of ending. Some stories are compelling and have difficult or sad endings. We also tend to enjoy those exciting, storybook endings where the underdog or the hero wins. One of my favorite movies combines both of those elements. At the memorable conclusion to *Avengers: Endgame*, Tony Stark makes a final self-sacrificing decision to defeat the enemy. He fought hard and made the ultimate decision to save others.

In the story of our own lives, we need to aspire to have those final chapters be filled with the kind of joy and hope experienced during amazing milestone moments and celebrations of previous decades. While aging undoubtedly includes many struggles, research suggests older adults often experience higher well-being in many ways compared to their younger peers.[10] Decide to persevere in pursuit of your purpose all the way through that finish line. Decide to finish the race well and make the most of each year of your one precious life, leaving a legacy that others can learn and draw inspiration from.

Don't be the one who counts the days to retirement for the sake of escaping work. Rather, see the exciting time of retirement as an opportunity to invest time and energy anew to fulfill your purpose. For those who can and plan to retire from full-time work, it is not only the end of one phase, but also, as noted previously, this significant ending means it is the beginning of another phase! The number of those approaching retirement age is as high as it's ever been. This "Peak 65" phenomenon is expected to continue for the next few years, which means there is amazing energy, experience, and wisdom with some freed-up hours in the day that could be shared with others!

Your finite energy will ebb and flow over time. In your young adult years, you will have more energy, but wisdom and experience are in a period of rapid growth. In our middle-aged years, our energy—at least for some of us—has stabilized, and our experience, and we hope wisdom, too, is on the rise. In our senior years, while energy levels may wane, experience and wisdom have been enriched, and it is so important to share that experience and wisdom with the next generation, so they will have a head start, accomplishing even greater contributions to benefit themselves and others.

---

10   Loren A. Olson, "To Be Happier, Start Thinking Like an Old Person," *Psychology Today*, July 21, 2023, https://www.psychologytoday.com/us/blog/finally-out/202307/to-be-happy-think-like-an-old-person.

While you may retire from work, you should never retire from pursuing your life on purpose. If you can retire at some point in your life, you may free up as many as forty or even more hours during your week. It is exciting to think about the other priorities in your life where you could spend that time. The possibilities are so immense to mentor formally and informally, develop others, impart wisdom in structured and unstructured environments, and continue to learn and experience new things.

The importance of living a life on purpose and leaving a legacy that is motivating to the next generation is particularly magnified in your later years. Some of the most impactful things I witnessed from my great-grandparents were things they did in their later years. It was so empowering to see them serve and care for others. Writers spend so much effort crafting a perfect ending to a story to keep readers fully engaged, anticipating what the finale is. Your life of purpose is worth similarly careful and intentional planning and spending quality effort to craft the ways that you want to cement your legacy. It is so tempting to rest because you feel you've earned it, but as one busy, high-energy senior joked, "I don't want to slow down. I can rest when I die!" Know that living your life on purpose has more—not less—importance and value in your senior years. So, if you've picked up this book and you are a senior, guess what? It is a perfect time to solidify that purpose and develop habits around your priorities, where you can fulfill your purpose and begin transferring a positive and motivating legacy to others.

Pick Up the Pace

Whatever point you find yourself at in your life, start now to live your life on purpose. Identify and honor your priorities, write your purpose statement, and begin in earnest to create habits that ensure you are making progress on your eternal, transcendent, and universal purpose. If you choose not to do that, your later years may expose that you've lived a life that defaulted to those things that simply filled your time and energy. Be ready to push against things that command your attention and time and know that you can choose to be the architect of your life. You can choose to live your life on purpose in an authentic way.

If you find yourself in your later years having lived a life in a less-than-purposeful way, you can absolutely still finish that race well and create the legacy you want. For those who started sooner, you have the opportunity to run a distance race, picking up the pace in those later decades. You can come right up to that starting line and run a meaningful sprint to the finish! That means every attentional moment and minute is a new opportunity to share your experience, lessons learned, and wisdom with others. There will undoubtedly be places for you to live your life on purpose in a way that motivates and inspires others.

A cherished memory for me was playing cards as a teenager with my grandfather. He loved cards, and he enjoyed using card games to connect with his grandchildren. I learned many lessons in those precious moments over holidays and breaks. First, he taught me the basics: the rules of the game, how to hold my cards, and how to shuffle the deck. It was fun and I learned to think strategically, pay attention to detail, and picked up a little eye-hand coordination, too! But I also learned how to participate and engage, how to play and win, and play and lose. I learned that using your skills rather than cheating to get the outcome you want is far more rewarding. In one game, I cheated because I knew I was not going to win. My grandfather halted the game right then and there. He taught me a lesson that was important and powerful. He helped me to understand that my character was far more valuable to the quality of my life than either winning or losing, and that it is better to lose with your character intact than to sacrifice it in order to win. Your character can be lost in an instant and it is much harder to win back. This attentional moment where he took the time and intentionally steered my mind and my heart was transformational for me.

It is too easy to overlook those within our sphere of influence, and again, while we're more digitally connected than ever, it is difficult to really get to know people. That message from my grandfather was so meaningful because my grandfather understood that I loved to compete. He also knew I had recently gained a newfound faith and he understood the importance of my professed faith aligning with my character. He could have judged me, simply quit the game, told my parents, or worse, said nothing. But I'm grateful that he cared enough about me and my future to pause, empathetically instruct, and speak into my life. It was an important point in my life, and I reflect on that conversation often.

We need to sprint to the finish, pursuing our purpose with diligence to cement a legacy. It is so tempting—really at any point in our lives—to want to focus on ourselves and yearn for simple, uncomplicated days. Those in and of themselves are not necessarily bad, but be sure to use that simpler life cadence as space to share, to mentor, to impart encouragement and wisdom for the next generation. I hope you've had the privilege of being with seniors whose stories, insights, and wisdom you simply couldn't get enough of.

My high school wrestling coach called me "the heart attack kid." I was not the best wrestler on the team. I didn't have the best technique or any skillset that set me apart from the other athletes. However, I never quit and always finished strong. Whether there was one minute left or one second left, I gave every ounce of energy I had on the mat. So, whether I won or lost, I knew that I had shared 100 percent of what I had that day. Sometimes expending that effort relentlessly throughout the match resulted in an unexpected win—hence the nickname! But of course, it didn't always result in a "W." However, I always knew that I'd lived my life on purpose in the best way I could in the moment.

The older we get, the more we understand how finite our time and energy truly are. We need to learn to live a life on purpose by sprinting hard to the finish. I've often heard it said that you can't take your money, assets, or possessions with you when you die. Some use that to make the case that you should enjoy it and others say you should share it. We likewise cannot take our experience, lessons learned, and wisdom with us either. So likewise, it makes sense to share them, too. My hope and my prayer is that you will remember the end of this book and commit to live a life on purpose. That you will intentionally build a legacy, leaving a mark indelibly on the lives of those you leave behind one day.

No matter where you are in your journey to live a life on purpose, you can begin that journey immediately. Do you just need to leave it all on the proverbial mat and get more intentional about your purpose? Do you need to find that passion and infuse it into each minute, moment, meeting, day, week, and year? Is it time to craft your eternal, transcendent, and universal purpose statement, so you can focus on a long-term vision for yourself and a legacy of purpose for the next generation? I truly hope that you will join me in living a life on purpose and begin to change the world one meaningful moment at a time!

Personal Purpose Inventory: Questions for Your Annual Checkpoint

1. **What is the most vivid aspect of your long-term vision?**

    _____

    _____

2. **What is one moment this year that best illustrates that long-term vision in action?**

    _____

    _____

3. **What is one thing you learned this year that helped you make progress on your purpose? What is one thing you want to learn next year?**

    _____

    _____

4. **Where were you when you felt most excited about your purpose this year? What were you doing?**

    _____

    _____

5. **What is one thing you have accomplished toward your five-year milestone?**

    _____

    _____

6. **What is one area you think you fell short?**

    _____

    _____

7. **Who helped you along the way this year? Who could help you next year?**

    _____

    _____

8. **Next year, what would you hope to do or achieve that will bring you closer to your five-year milestone?**

    _____

    _____

About the Author

Photo by Elise Nyffeler

Reed Nyffeler is a lifelong entrepreneur with a passion for developing the next generation of leaders, finding solutions, and implementing growth strategies. As the CEO and founder of Signal, he has led the fast-growing, industry-leading security services franchisor with a mission to provide peace of mind to pursue passion in life. Through intentionality grounded in an unshakeable faith, Nyffeler has learned to identify his priorities and to passionately pursue his purpose in every area of his life. He carefully balances his professional aspirations with time spent enjoying and connecting with his happy, thriving family of six.